Gholsons in Early America

And Their Connections With the Founding Fathers

Gholsons in Early America

And Their Connections With the Founding Fathers

~

Compiled and Edited by
Donna Gholson Cook

ABOOKS
Alive Book Publishing

Gholsons in Early America
And Their Connections with The Founding Fathers
Copyright © 2020 by Donna Gholson Cook

Additional copies may be ordered from the publisher for educational, business,
promotional or premium use. For information, contact ALIVE Book Publishing at:
alivebookpublishing.com, or call (925) 837-7303.

ISBN 13
978-1-63132-103-0

Library of Congress Control Number: 2020915207
Library of Congress Cataloging-in-Publication Data is available upon request.

First Edition

Published in the United States of America by ALIVE Book Publishing and
ALIVE Publishing Group, imprints of Advanced Publishing LLC
3200 A Danville Blvd., Suite 204, Alamo, California 94507
alivebookpublishing.com

PRINTED IN THE UNITED STATES OF AMERICA

10 9 8 7 6 5 4 3 2 1

Other books by Donna Gholson Cook

Gholson Road—Revolutionaries and Texas Rangers 2004

*Fritz and Annie Lippe Family—German Cotton Farmers
in Early 1900s Texas* 2009

Annie's Story—Memories of my Grandmother 2017

*Gholson Brothers In the Thick of It—True Stories of Early Texas as Told
by Two Who Lived It* 2019

Dedicated to all Descendants of
Anthony Gholson of Virginia and Kentucky
and his wife, Elizabeth (Sandidge) Gholson

Our family has a rich history
with many connections to the
American Revolution, the
War of 1812, and the Founding Fathers
of our great nation.

Let us not forget them.

Contents

Illustrations

~

Maps

Gholson Line

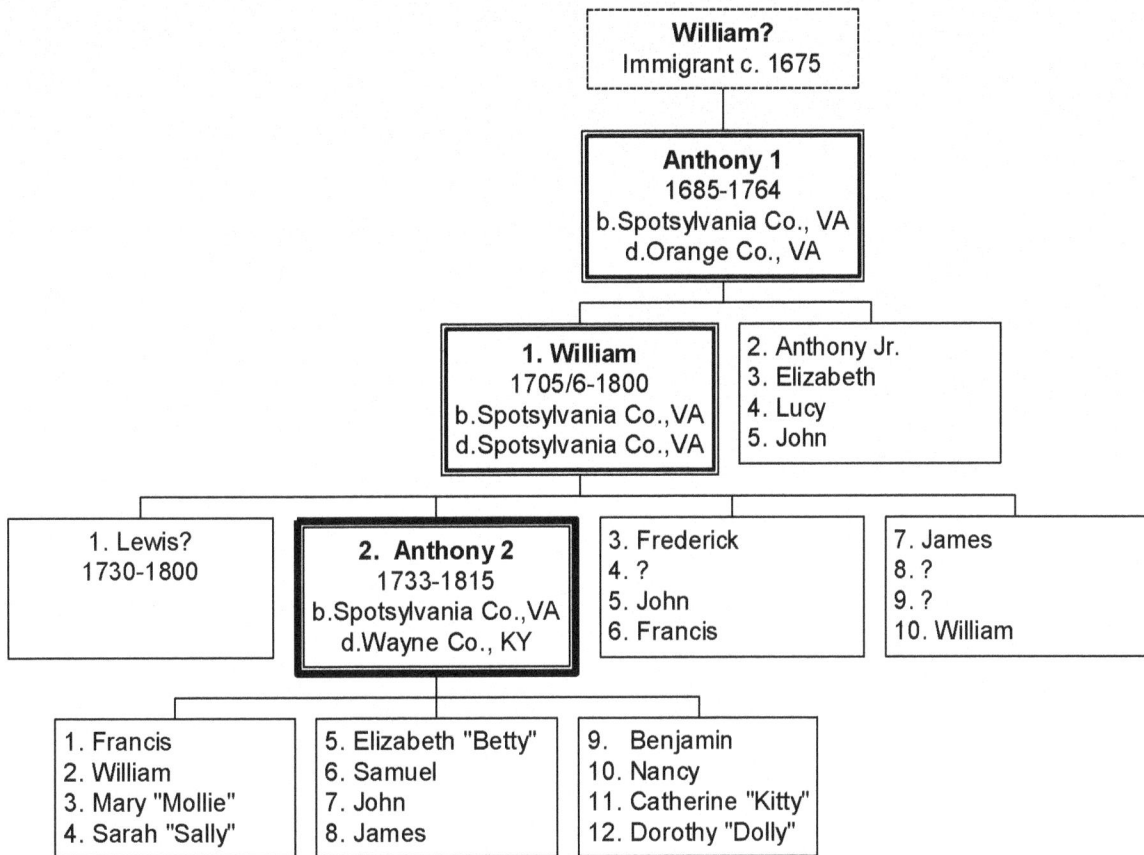

William?
Immigrant c. 1675

Anthony 1
1685-1764
b.Spotsylvania Co., VA
d.Orange Co., VA

1. William
1705/6-1800
b.Spotsylvania Co.,VA
d.Spotsylvania Co.,VA

2. Anthony Jr.
3. Elizabeth
4. Lucy
5. John

1. Lewis?
1730-1800

2. Anthony 2
1733-1815
b.Spotsylvania Co.,VA
d.Wayne Co., KY

3. Frederick
4. ?
5. John
6. Francis

7. James
8. ?
9. ?
10. William

1. Francis
2. William
3. Mary "Mollie"
4. Sarah "Sally"

5. Elizabeth "Betty"
6. Samuel
7. John
8. James

9. Benjamin
10. Nancy
11. Catherine "Kitty"
12. Dorothy "Dolly"

~

This chart is a compilation of information from many sources, and every effort was made to verify and use the best references available. There are many versions of the names and number of children in these large families. The separation of the children of **Anthony₂** and his wife **Elizabeth** is only for the purpose of showing oldest, middle, and youngest groups.

DGC

Introduction

Stories of my Gholson ancestors have fascinated me since I was very young, and when I realized that their stories are preserved in many different libraries, I began to research them. I wanted to share the stories with other Gholson descendants, so in 2004 I published my first book, ***Gholson Road—Revolutionaries and Texas Rangers***. I have been asked how I found information on the Gholson family going back hundreds of years. Fortunately, the name "Gholson" is fairly uncommon, and I had a 1950 book, ***Gholson and Allied Families***, by Virginia Baker Mitchell, to use as a starting point for dates and places of births, deaths, marriages, and military information. Then my real search began.

I have spent many hours in public libraries, especially those with a good genealogy collection. If I found myself in another city with some time on my hands, I headed for the library. I first searched the catalog for names and keywords based upon the information I already had. It always amazed me to find Gholson information in every library I visited, as far away as Toronto, Canada. As I became more familiar with my subjects, I browsed through the shelves for books covering topics that looked as though they might be useful, such as deed records of early Virginia, or muster rolls of the Kentucky militia. Each time I found a reference to the Gholson name in a book, I photocopied the appropriate pages, including the title page and copyright information for the book.

In searching for the first Gholson immigrants from England, I began checking the early ships' records for variations on the Gholson name, found in a Boston library. In the early records, names were often spelled very creatively, since many people could neither read nor write even their own names, and it was often a challenge for the person who recorded the name to attempt to spell it phonetically.

In the course of my research, I made several interesting discoveries, such as 1728 Virginia land grants from King George II, a family connection to Patrick Henry, and a reference to land leased from George Washington by my Gholson ancestor who failed to pay his rent on time. My husband Lew enjoys telling people that I qualify for the D.A.R.—Deadbeats of the American Revolution! In doing my research, the history of our nation became very real to me when I realized the close connection between my 4th great-grandfather in Virginia and our Founding Fathers. I checked land records, courthouse records, military records, criminal records, and anything else that seemed to have possibilities. Since there were often several Gholsons with the same name, such as Anthony and William, I was careful to match dates and places with individuals. I collected many maps, topographic maps, land grant maps, etc., and included portions of them in my books.

The amount of information I found soon became a bit overwhelming, so to organize it, I made a spreadsheet showing dates chronologically in the first column, starting with the oldest. The second column contained historical events, especially those occurring near the family's residence at that time (for instance, the Revolutionary War was taking place when they lived in Virginia). Next, there is a column for each generation. The spreadsheet tells me at a glance what historical events were taking place on any significant family history date and the number of years of overlap between generations. Paying attention to the birth and death dates helps to sort out the generations who were named after their father or grandfather.

So that is the capsule version of how I collected and organized information about the Gholson family line from my great-grandfather, Benjamin Franklin Gholson, one of the first Texas Rangers, back to early Virginia and England. Finally, the chapters began to emerge and the book began to take shape. Now that I had an idea of who, where, and when, I became curious about what life was like for the various family members. I began to search for material to describe the times, and blended it with the family history information. By the time the first draft was finished, I was much more familiar with the lives and times of my ancestors and had a good refresher course in American and Texas history. I would have enjoyed my school history classes a lot more if I had known that I had ancestors who were alive and involved in the events! Since 2004 when *Gholson Road* was published, I have discovered new information and took a road trip through the areas in Virginia and Kentucky where they lived, so I decided to publish another book focusing on the early Gholsons in the early years of America. I hope you enjoy reading it as much as I have enjoyed gathering the information and assembling it!

Donna Gholson Cook
www.gholson-cook.com

Timeline

1500-1599:

1500 Voyages of discovery by Columbus, Cabot, Vasco da Gama, Magellan

1517 The Reformation

1572 **Dr. Theodore Gulston** born

1578 Humphrey Gilbert obtained charter from Queen Elizabeth to colonize

1585 Walter Raleigh established Virginia

1588 England defeated the Spanish Armada

1596 Will proved in England mentioned **Anthony Goulson**

1600-1699:

1604 King James I of England made peace treaty with Spain

1606 Virginia Company of London created

1607 Settlement of Jamestown began

1610 **Dr. Gulston** received doctor's degree at Oxford

1616 **Dr. Gulston** entertained Sir Thomas Dale and Powhatan's counsellor

1619 **Dr. Gulston** bought ten shares in the Virginia Company

1620 **Dr. Gulston** was made one of the King's Council for the Company

1620 The *Mayflower* sailed from Holland

1621 **Dr. Gulston** recommended Dr. Pott for physician-general of Virginia

1622 347 Virginians massacred by Indians

1624 Population of Virginia was 1292

1624 Virginia was converted into a Royal Colony

1629 King Charles I dissolved Parliament in England

1632 **Dr. Theodore Gulston** died at home in St. Martin's on Ludgate Hill

1632 Seventeen laws passed in Virginia - Church of England

1634 **Dr. Gulston's** brother **John** was a Justice of the Peace in England

1634 **Henry Gouldson** and family left England for America

1641 **Anthony Gunston** transported to America by John Bayly (Bayles)

1642 Sir William Berkeley arrived in Virginia

1644 Indian attack

1670 Increase in the number of slaves

1670 Plows came into use

1671 Governor Berkeley opposes educating the common people

1675 **William₁ Goulston** listed in shippers by the *Joanna* from London for Virginia

1685 **Anthony₁ Gholson** born in Spotsylvania County about this time

1700-1799:

1705 **Anthony₁'s** son **William₂** born

1716 Virginia's Royal Governor Spotswood led his party out of Williamsburg to claim the Appalachian mountains for England and to stop the advance of the French in the interior

1725 **Anthony₁'s** first recorded transaction of a purchase of 200 acres in Spotsylvania County, St. George Parish, in 1725

1727-1733 **Anthony₁ Gholson** was caretaker and overseer of the road in Spotsylvania County

1728 **Anthony₁** obtained a grant from King George II for 1000 acres on Terry's Run in Spotsylvania County (see Appendix 1); sons **Anthony, Jr.** and **William₂** received grants at the same time

1729 **Anthony₁** summoned by Grand Jury for not revealing a bastard child

1733 **Anthony₂ (William₂'s** son) born around this time

1738 **Anthony₁** had sold all of the 1000 acres

1739 **Anthony₁** and his wife Jane sold the 200 acres to Zachary Lewis

1740 **Anthony₁** bought 400 acres from John Chew and wife

1744 **Anthony₁** named as guardian to Hannah Durram

1744 **Anthony₁** sold 120 acres

1747-1774 **William₂** bought and sold many tracts of land

1750   Joseph Collins took the oath as Captain of a Troop of Horse

1750   Voyage horrors described by Gottfried Mittelberger

1754-63 French and Indian War

1756 Collins' troop joined the Culpeper County Militia to fight the Indians above Winchester

1757 Joseph Collins died

1760-1786 Twelve children born to **Anthony₂** and wife **Elizabeth**

1760 **Francis Gholson** born, son of **Anthony₂** and **Elizabeth**

1761 **Anthony₁** sold the remaining 280 acres

1763 **Anthony₁** executed deeds of gift

1764 **Anthony₁** died; wife **Jane** executed deed of gift

1764 **William³ Gholson** born, son of **Anthony₂** and **Elizabeth**

1765 Stamp Act

1766 **Mary "Mollie" Gholson** born, daughter of **Anthony₂** and **Elizabeth**

1767 Tax on tea

1768 **Sarah "Sally" Gholson** born, daughter of **Anthony₂** and **Elizabeth**

1767 Tax on tea

1768-1786 **Anthony₂** rented land from George Washington in Frederick County

1769 Daniel Boone left Virginia to go hunting in Kentucky - May 1

1770 Boston Massacre

1770 **Elizabeth "Betty" Gholson** born, daughter of **Anthony₂** and **Elizabeth**

1770-71 Daniel Boone and his brother spent the winter hunting, trapping and exploring in southern Kentucky

1771 Daniel Boone and brother left Kentucky for home in March

1771 Letter written by George Washington to his brother Samuel Washington discussing the best way to collect **Anthony₂ Gholson's** rent

1772 **Samuel Gholson** born, son of **Anthony₂** and **Elizabeth**

1773 Daniel Boone and other families left Clinch River area to move to Kentucky - turned back by Indian attack

1774 Request to English Parliament to repeal acts passed in previous decade

1775 **John Gholson** born 8 February, son of **Anthony₂** and **Elizabeth**

1775 Daniel Boone led a party to blaze a trail through the wilderness

1775 Patrick Henry's speech - March 23

1775 Colonel Henderson left for Kentucky following Boone trail March 28

1775 Paul Revere's ride - April 18

1775 Battle of Lexington, beginning of Revolutionary War - April 19

1775 Henderson's party arrived at Fort Boone - April 20

1775 Patrick Henry confronts Lord Dunmore - April 28

1775 Lord Dunmore reconvened the House of Burgesses - May

1775 Washington appointed general and commander in chief of Continental troops - June 15

1775 **Anthony₂** signed petition in Berkeley County, West Virginia, protesting an election

1775-1786 **William's** first wife, **Susannah (Collins)** died during this time

1776 **James Gholson** born 26 September, son of **Anthony₂** and **Elizabeth**

1776 Henderson's request denied to have Kentucky admitted as 14ᵗʰ colony

1776 Jefferson was asked to draft the Declaration of Independence

1776 Declaration of Independence approved by Congress - July 4

1777 **J. Benjamin Gholson** born, son of **Anthony₂** and **Elizabeth**

1778 **Nancy Gholson** born, daughter of **Anthony₂** and **Elizabeth**

1778 **Anthony₂** lived in Beverley Manor, Augusta County, Virginia, where he bought 374 acres

1779 **Anthony₂** had sold the 374 acres and moved to Botetourt County - court martial summons issued for **Anthony₂**, for missing Augusta County militia musters

1780 **Catherine "Kitty" Gholson** born, daughter of **Anthony₂** and **Elizabeth**

1780 **Anthony₂ Gholson** received a grant of 992 acres in Kentucky

1780 Virginia invaded by British forces led by Benedict Arnold

1780-1801 Numerous land transactions for **Anthony₂** in Botetourt

1781 Richmond captured and burned by second British invasion - January

1781 Battle of Guilford Court House

1782 **Francis**, son of **Anthony₂** and **Elizabeth**, married **Mary Craig**

1783 **Anthony₂** served on a jury

1783 **Anthony₂** purchased 200 acres in Fayette County

1784 **William³**, son of **Anthony₂** and **Elizabeth**, married **Mary Cross**

1784 **Anthony₂** purchased 680 acres

1784 House built for reception of deer skins and hemp, which were accepted as payment of taxes in Botetourt County, with **Anthony₂** appointed as inspector

1785 **Anthony₂** bought 1000 acres

1785 **Micah Taul** born

1785-1788 **Anthony₂** was surveyor of the road

1786 **Dorothy "Dolly" Gholson** born, daughter of **Anthony₂** and **Elizabeth**

1788 **Mary "Mollie,"** daughter of **Anthony₂** and **Elizabeth**, married **Joseph Chrisman**

1788 **Sarah "Sally,"** daughter of **Anthony₂** and **Elizabeth**, married **Isaac Chrisman**

1789 **Elizabeth "Betty,"** daughter of **Anthony₂** and **Elizabeth**, married twice, first to **James Neely**, second to **William Neely** in 1789

1790 **Anthony₂** sold 1000 acres

1790-1800 **Anthony₂** assembled 1180 acre plantation

1792 Kentucky became the 15ᵗʰ state of the Union

1792 Postal service extended to Kentucky in August

1792 **Anthony₂** was overseer of the road

1793 **Anthony₂** built a new gristmill

1794 **Anthony₂** obtained permit for another gristmill

1794 **John**, son of **Anthony₂** and **Elizabeth**, married **Lucretia Griffith**

1796 New Wilderness Road completed

1796 **James**, son of **Anthony₂** and **Elizabeth**, married **Martha "Patsy" Lewis**

1800-1829:

1800 **William₂** died about this time

1800-1801 Wayne County, Kentucky, established

1801 **Anthony₂** sold 1180 acres in Virginia

1801 **Anthony₂**, with family and slaves, crossed the mountains to Kentucky from Virginia – he was one of the founders of the town of Monticello

1801 **Anthony₂** donated land for the construction of a Baptist church

1801 **Micah Taul** elected first county clerk of Wayne County - March 16

1801 **Samuel,** son of **Anthony₂** and **Elizabeth,** married **Mary Ann "Polly" Slaton**

1801 **Catherine "Kitty,"** daughter of **Anthony₂** and **Elizabeth,** married **Bartholomew Hayden**

1802 **Dorothy "Dolly"** daughter of **Anthony₂** and **Elizabeth,** married **Micah Taul**

1802 **Anthony₂** purchased 105-acre tract in Wayne County

1803 **J. Benjamin Gholson**, son of **Anthony₂** and **Elizabeth**, married **Mary "Polly" Hayden**

1803 Louisiana purchase ratified

1804 **Anthony₂** helped to organize Big Sinking Baptist Church

1807 **Anthony₂** purchased 220-acre tract

1812 War declared against Britain June 18

1812 Kentucky volunteers reported for duty - August

1812 Hull surrendered Fort Detroit - August 16

1812 Chauncey was placed in command of the American naval forces on Erie and Ontario - September

1812 Chauncey turned Lake Erie over to young Commodore Perry

1813 Deeds of gift signed by **Anthony₂**

1813 **Taul's** troops returned home - March

1813 Kentucky troops called up again in June, to rendezvous in August

1813 Perry defeated British fleet in Battle of Lake Erie - September 10

1813 **Taul's** company, including **Samuel Gholson**, arrived at Lake Erie

1813 Battle of the Thames - October 5

1813 Tribes signed armistice agreement with General Harrison - October 16

1814 **Micah Taul** elected to Congress

1814 Defeat of Napoleon in the spring allowed Britain to focus on America

1814 British burned the White House - August 24

1814 British attacked Fort McHenry - September 14

1814 **Samuel Gholson** enlisted in Captain Vickery's company Nov. 10

1814 Treaty of Ghent ended War of 1812 - December 24

1815 **Anthony₂** donated land for Baptist church and cemetery at Steubenville

1815 Battle of New Orleans - January 8

1815 **Anthony₂** died

One: The Immigrants

Anthony₁ of Virginia c. 1685 - c. 1764
William₂ of Virginia c. 1705 - c. 1795-1800

World Changing Events
First, let us have a brief look at world events when the first Europeans were coming to the American continent. The Italian Renaissance marked the end of the Middle Ages. The printing press made the newly-accumulated knowledge more accessible, resulting in a more educated population. The voyages of discovery around 1500 by Columbus, Cabot, Vasco da Gama, and Magellan provided hope for new places to live and a new way of life. The Reformation began in 1517 when a German priest named Martin Luther challenged corrupt practices of the Church authorities at a time when the Church was the temporal and religious authority. The work of scholars such as Copernicus and Galileo revolutionized commonly held scientific beliefs. All of these factors, along with increased difficulty in trading with the East, added momentum to the desire to go to the newly-discovered American continent, the source of unlimited wealth. At the same time, the flow of products and silver into Europe from America caused extreme inflation and made life in the Old World more and more difficult.[1]

Dr. Theodore Gulston's England
Theodore Gulston was a child in England in 1578 when an Englishman named Humphrey Gilbert recognized the possibility of colonizing the new lands and obtained a charter from Queen Elizabeth to begin. Unfortunately, Gilbert died when his ship sank, but his half-brother Walter Raleigh carried on alone, establishing in 1585 a colony that he called Virginia, in honor of the queen. That attempt did not succeed, nor did one two years later, and then England became too preoccupied with the Spanish War to try again for another twenty years.[2] In 1588, England defeated the Spanish Armada in a naval battle that launched England as a world power, but the struggle between England and Spain continued, as did the competition for the New World.[3] In 1604, England's King James I made a peace treaty with Spain, giving England the opportunity to again turn its attention to the colonization of America.[4]

There were many reasons for the English to migrate to America. With the worsening situation caused by inflation, excessive regulation of industry by the government, the difficulty in joining the craftsmen's guilds, and the peasants being driven off the land, more and more people were becoming unable to support themselves and their families.[5] Most emigrants came from the middle and lower-middle classes, although class distinction was less pronounced in America than it had been in England. Most were not farmers before they moved to America.[6] They may have to come to America for religious freedom, economic or other reasons, but there was one thing that they did not want to change—they wanted to remain Englishmen and to recreate the culture they left behind. Some of them did not like the changes taking place in England and saw America as a place where they could retain old customs.[7] They brought with them farming tools, livestock, seeds, chests full of personal belongings, and a determination to recreate England in the wilderness of America.[8] To their surprise, instead of a wilderness, they found large fields which had been cleared and planted in corn by the Indians, although not many Indians had survived the smallpox epidemic spread by European fishermen.[9] The Indians were generally helpful, but in Virginia they were more numerous and posed a greater threat than in New England.[10]

English merchants began to realize that there were opportunities to make money in the new land and they began to pool their resources to form joint stock companies. In 1606, the Virginia Company of London was created. In May 1607, the settlement of Jamestown was begun. In a year, half of the several hundred settlers were dead, but those remaining were eventually able to support themselves. Captain John Smith became the leader of the colony and the "marriage of his lieutenant John Rolfe with Pocahontas, the daughter of the Indian chief Powhatan, caused a sensation in the English capital."[11] Powhatan managed to maintain peace between his people and the colonists, but after his death in 1618, his warlike brother conducted raids upon the settlements, which began a cycle of war resulting in the end of the Powhatan Confederacy.[12]

Fig. 1.1 - *Portrait of Pocahontas*, photograph of a painting in the United States Capitol, copied from original by William Sheppard, dated 1616, at Barton rectory, Norfolk, England. Detroit Publishing Co. No. M 18753. Gift; State Historical Society of Colorado; 1949, Library of Congress No. LC-D416-18753.

Dr. Theodore Gulston, believed to be related to the first members of the Gholson family in America,[13]

> . . . was a celebrated London physician and a prominent member of the Virginia Company. He was born in 1572, studied at Merton College, Oxford, where he took his doctor's degree, April 30, 1610, was fellow (Dec. 29, 1611,) and Censor of the College of Physicians, and practised with great success in London. In 1616 he frequently entertained Sir Thomas Dale and Uttomakin, Powhatan's counsellor, who had been sent to England. On June 14, 1619, ***Dr. Gulston*** was appointed on the committee of the Virginia Company in regard to the college. On Dec. 15, 1619, he bought ten shares of land in Virginia from various persons. He was made one of the King's Council for the Company in England, on July 8, 1620, and in July 1621, he recommended Dr. Pott for appointment as physician-general of Virginia. ***Dr. Gulston*** was distinguished as a Greek and Latin scholar, and translated several works from Greek into Latin.[14]

Dr. Gulston was also the founder of the Gulstonian lecture series at the College of Physicians, Cambridge.[15] His name is listed frequently in the *Records of the Virginia Company of London* as an attendee at court sessions, beginning in May of 1619.[16]

Dr. Gulston's brother ***John*** was a Justice of the Peace in England in 1634.[17] At that time, justices of the peace were the law enforcers of the countryside in England and were the only people outside the armed forces who had the right to bear arms.[18] They were members of the gentry, appointed by the Crown. "The office could be an exasperating burden, but one few gentlemen dared to refuse; it was an honor to receive, a duty to accept, and a training ground for those eager to serve in Parliament."[19]

> A justice of the peace carried heavy administrative duties. He fixed wages, licensed alehouses and checked that they observed hours, apprenticed boys to trades, found homes for orphans, saw to the care of the poor and infirm, disciplined the obstreperous, inspected roads and bridges, punished all legal infractions, large and small. He kept, or was supposed to keep, the king's ministers informed on all aspects of local life that might be relevant to the welfare of the nation. The increasing number of impositions upon him from London under the early Stuarts convinced some

of the justices they had little to lose in moving to America. - David Freeman Hawke, *Everyday Life in Early America* [20]

Succeeding generations of Gholsons were road inspectors, surveyors, and were also involved in various phases of law enforcement. **John Gulston** married **Jane**, the daughter of Richard Ketridge, and they had eleven children, the youngest of whom was named **William**.[21] This **William** may have been the first member of the family to move to America.

Dr. Theodore Gulston died in his home in St. Martin's on Ludgate Hill on May 4, 1632.[22] In his will, he left a portion of his estate to his brother John's children.[23] Theodore's brother Nathaniel also had a son named William, but Nathaniel's son William lived a distinguished life in England and died there in 1684.[24] **John Gulston's** son **William** may have been the same **William Goulston** who was listed in shippers by the *Joanna* from London for Virginia in March 1675.[25] Since **Anthony₁** was born about ten years later, the timing would be about right for **William** to have been his father. In early Virginia, first-born children were often named for their grandparents, and second-born for parents.[26] Since the second son of **Anthony₁ Gholson** was named Anthony, after himself, and the first son's name is **William**, it is reasonable to assume that **Anthony₁'s** father was also named William.

Early Colonists & Horrific Voyages

The directors of the London company (also called the Virginia Company) had many ideas as to the source for profit from the new colonies, but none of them guessed that it would be tobacco. The smoking habit had been brought to England by the Spaniards and the demand for tobacco was just beginning when it was discovered that Virginia had an excellent soil and climate for growing it. The planters soon grew rich and as their wealth grew, their sense of independence increased.[27]

Also assisted by the Virginia company was a group of thirty-five Puritans who sailed from Holland in September 1620 with sixty-six adventurers on the *Mayflower*. Their patent was invalidated when they landed at Cape Cod two and a half months later because they were outside the jurisdiction of the Virginia company.[28] There was a disagreement about who would lead the two groups on board the *Mayflower*, considering their differences in goals and moral values, and the *Mayflower Compact* was drawn up "for the general good of the colony."[29] There was no lucrative crop in Massachusetts, as there had been in Virginia, resulting in no profits for the financial backers, but the colony survived.[30]

The colony of Massachusetts was established following the 1629 dissolution of Parliament in England by King Charles I and his Personal Rule. In the following ten years, the number of colonists grew to fourteen thousand, some of whom began moving out to start other colonies.[31]

Many of the early colonists were lured to America by an intense advertising campaign conducted through poems, pamphlets, sermons and any other media available. After the Indian massacre in Virginia in 1622 had dampened the enthusiasm of many prospective emigrants, the Reverend John Donne was paid in stock by the Virginia Company for preaching a sermon in which he "declared that continued support of the colony would advance both the interests of England and the Kingdom of God."[32] The advertising was apparently favorable enough to outweigh the many tales of horror on the other extreme, such as the rumor that New England had flying rattlesnakes that could kill a man by breathing on him.[33]

Most of the first immigrants to Virginia had origins in the southern and western parts of England.[34] Between 1606 and 1625, more than 5600 people left England to start a new life in Virginia. By 1625, only about 1100 remained alive.[35] The first big challenge was to survive the voyage. Gottfried Mittelberger described the conditions on one of the immigrant ships which landed in Philadelphia on October 10, 1750, in his *Journey to Pennsylvania.* "During the journey the ship is full of pitiful signs of distress—smells, fumes, horrors, vomiting, various kinds of sea sickness, fever, dysentery, headaches, heat, constipation, boils, scurvy, cancer, mouth-rot . . ."[36] There is a shortage of food and water. The water is "very black, thick with dirt, and full of worms."[37] The little bit of spoiled bread that is available is "full of red worms and spiders' nests."[38] There are "so many lice, especially on the sick people, that they have to be scraped off the bodies."[39] Small children seldom had the strength to survive the voyage, often dying from measles or smallpox.[40] To compound the misery, a storm would arise and for several days everyone on board was in fear that the ship would sink.[41] Even when land was finally reached, those who could not pay for the voyage were forced to remain on board until they were purchased, and those who were ill had little chance of that.[42]

Anthony₁ Gholson

In the years just before the Revolutionary War, there were many like **Anthony₁ Gholson's** family who had come to America at least a hundred years before but new settlers were arriving by the thousands.[43] Many of the English who came to Virginia in the early years were members of distinguished families but left because of the rule of primogeniture (inheritance of the family estate by the oldest son), hoping to improve their situation in America.[44]

The parents or grandparents of *Anthony₁ Gholson* of Virginia were on board one of those leaky little ships from England that arrived on the coast of America before Anthony₁ was born in Spotsylvania County around 1685. His father may have been *Dr. Theodore Gulston's nephew William.* Anthony₁ was probably a son or grandson of a pioneer because he signed his name with a capital "A" rather than a signature. If he had come directly from England, he would have probably been able to read and write, but the pioneers' constant battle for survival left little time for education.[45]

Others who may have been related to *Anthony₁'s* English ancestors include the following:

- On November 6, 1596, a will was proved in England, mentioning one Anthony Goulson among the friends of the deceased, John Davenaunte.[46]
- Henry Gouldson, age 43; Ann, his wife, age 45; Ann Gouldslon (*sic*), age 18; and Mary Gouldson, age 15 (probably the daughters of Henry and Ann), "took shipping in the *Elizabeth*, of Ipswich, Mr. William Andrews, bound for New England, the last of April 1634."[47]
- Antho. Gunston was one of fourteen persons transported by John Bayly (Bayles), who entered a claim for 700 acres (50 acres per head) on the north side of the Charles River on October 18, 1641.[48]

Immigrants paid a very high price

The new American colonists came from every nation in Europe, taking as much as two months to cross the ocean. At the end of a miserable and dangerous voyage, they found a land which contained abundance and opportunity, but they also faced hostile natives and fatal diseases not known in Europe. The first Europeans to come to America were mostly single men. If a wife was left behind in England, the man would send for her when settled and confident of being able to support a family. Since there were so few women in the colonies, those who were there had little trouble marrying well.[49]

More than forty percent of the Chesapeake area immigrants to America were indentured servants who were required to work for several years for whomever paid their passage. At the end of the indenture, they were free to live as they chose.[50] The master could buy or sell the indentured servant, or bequeath him as private property.[51] Most were young single working-class males,[52] but every occupation and profession was represented in this group—laborers, schoolteachers, craftsmen, doctors. While they endured hardships, they could look forward to a freedom from their bondage in a few years. On the dark side of the indenture system, many parents traded their children's freedom for their own. The children were bonded servants until the age of twenty-one and often did not see their parents for years, if ever.[53] The indentured servants supported the society in the North. The Southern equivalent of the indentured servant was the multitude of slaves brought by shiploads from Africa[54] who had to endure much more horrible conditions than the colonists who came voluntarily.[55] There were also prisoners sent to America because of the overcrowded prisons in England.[56]

As to terminology, the settlers who came to America from the British countries were called "imports" and were automatically citizens. Those who came from countries considered "foreign," such as Germany, were "immigrants" and had to become naturalized.[57] The first wave of colonists through the first half of the seventeenth century was predominantly English, but they were followed by Scotch-Irish, German and French settlers. There was enough land for everyone and the westward movement was beginning.[58] They were developing an independent streak in which the seed was germinating that would later result in the American Revolution.

Two: Life in Early Virginia
1600-1800

Anthony₁ of Virginia c. 1685 - c. 1764
William of Virginia c. 1705 - c. 1795-1800
Anthony₂ b. 1733 Virginia, moved to Kentucky 1801, died 1815

To the colonists who survived the voyage, America must have seemed like heaven on earth after the horror stories they had been told about what they would encounter in the new land. There was an abundance of wild fruits and berries, huge flocks of wild turkeys, thousands of ducks, and rivers and streams filled with fish. Unfortunately, the colonists were too ill and exhausted from the voyage and too poorly equipped to take advantage of the abundance. Most of them had no guns for hunting. Vacant land, streams, and wood were plentiful, and these three things "worked together slowly to transform the Englishman into something he did not plan on—a new breed of man."[1]

> America might be a land of promise, but "the promise was to the diligent rather than to the adventuresome." There was wood for fires, but he must first "cut and fetch it home" before he could burn it. There was wood for housing, but he "must build his house before he would have it." In short, men had in America "all things to do, as in the beginning of the world," and one of the first things to do was clear the land. – David Freeman Hawke, *Everyday Life in Early America* [2]

The farmers were also limited by their simple and inefficient tools. It was more than a hundred years before any real improvements were made and tools such as scythes and axes approached the quality seen today. Plows did not become common until the 1670s.[3] The most useful crop was corn, which the settlers learned how to grow from the Indians, and no part of the plant was wasted, even the husks, which were used to stuff mattresses.[4] In addition to the dishes made from corn (called *maize* by the Indians), the settlers had kitchen gardens and fruit trees, usually apple and peach. While there were some chickens and goats brought from England, the hog was the staple meat. The hogs ran loose in the woods and when they were butchered, no part of them was wasted.[5] Cattle were highly valued and became the first industry for American farmers,[6] but protecting them from rustlers and wolves was difficult.[7]

Farmhouses in seventeenth-century America usually consisted of a hall at the ground level with a loft above for sleeping and storage space. There was no kitchen, bathroom, or closets. Cooking and eating were done in the downstairs hall and all family members used an outhouse.[8] "In the Chesapeake more than half the households contained personal belongings worth less than sixty pounds."[9] The family ate from a long board, hence the expression "room and board."[10] If the family was prosperous, they might own a bedstead or two, which was kept in the hall. As many as a dozen family members might live in this small area, from infants to elderly, and the style of living changed very little for two hundred years.[11]

The necessity to move frequently to a new area usually meant that the seventeenth century tobacco planters lived in a hovel, because all of their energy went into making a large cash crop of tobacco. Gardens and orchards were neglected, and the planters often did not plant enough corn to feed the family through the winter. "Those who charged him with laziness failed to note that he grew the most demanding crop produced in colonial America."[12] From February to October, the seeds were planted, transplanted, kept free of weeds and pests, cut, hung in sheds to dry, taken down, the leaves stripped and pressed into hogsheads, weighing between 1000 and 1300 pounds. All of the year's chores were done in the next three months—building fences, clearing fields, and cutting firewood.[13]

Robert Beverley, an early Virginia historian, kept an excellent and thorough record of the world around him. He wrote about the song of the mockingbirds and the beautifully colored hummingbirds flocking around the honeysuckle. He described the summer thunderstorms and the wonderful smell of the woods.[14] He mentioned finding a bullfrog that was so large that "six French-Men might have made a comfortable Meal of its Carcase."[15] He found very little wrong with Virginia and downplayed the three things that he found annoying—thunder, heat and vermin. He had a remedy for every minor nuisance, such as mosquitoes or "musketaes" and ticks.[16] Beverley attributed most of the illnesses of people to their own poor judgment. Either they ate too much fruit, they dressed too warmly, or they became too damp and chilled. He credited the good health of the population to the use of herbal remedies and, interestingly enough, to the shortage of doctors. ". . . there is not Mystery enough, to make a Trade of Physick there, as the Learned do in other Countries, to the great oppression of Mankind."[17]

Doctors & medicine

In reality there were medical professionals sent to the colonies by the London Company and their fees were considered exhorbitant even in 1655, but a large part of the fee was for the time spent in travelling to the patients, unlike those in England.[18]

Another innovation broke more sharply with English medical traditions. There medical practice was divided into three branches—the physician, addressed as "doctor," who was a university graduate with a sound grounding in medical theory; the surgeon, addressed as "mister," who was considered little more than a craftsman; and the apothecary, who compounded and sold drugs. All three came to America in the early ships and tried to practice as they had at home. The cumbersome arrangement collapsed quickly, and for a simple reason—there was not enough business in the thinly populated land to keep all three fully employed. By the end of the century the American doctor served as physician to his patients, did his own surgery, and concocted his own drugs. - David Freeman Hawke, *Everyday Life in Early America* [19]

The mortality rate in Virginia was high—twice that of rural Massachusetts, with about half of all children dying before they became adults.[20] Many diseases as they were described at the time are difficult to identify today, but malaria and smallpox are identifiable by the symptoms. There was an outbreak of smallpox every ten or fifteen years, as new generations of susceptible children were born. The resulting deaths were slow and horrible, with the whole body breaking out in sores which stuck to the bed when the patient turned over, leaving large patches of skin behind. Smallpox killed hundreds of Indians and settlers alike.[21] Fever was cured by bleeding the patient, then purging the intestines.[22] Rattlesnakes were used in many cures, such as cooking the flesh in a broth and feeding it to the patient, mixing its gall with chalk for stomach aches, and using its oil for gout.[23] Starvation caused some of the early colonists to become cannibals.[24]

Due to the frequent epidemics of deadly diseases, orphaned children were common, and there was hardly a household that did not include one or more of these children.

In tidewater Virginia during the seventeenth century, most children—more than three-quarters, in fact—lost at least one parent before reaching the age of eighteen. One consequence was to enlarge the importance of other kin; for when a nuclear family was broken in Virginia the extended family picked up the pieces. Another consequence was to change the structure of the household in a fundamental way. Historians Darrett and Anita Rutman observe that in "just about any" household one might find "orphans, half-brother, stepbrothers and stepsisters, and wards running a gamut of ages. The father figure in the house might well be an uncle or a brother, the mother figure an aunt, elder sister, or simply the father's 'now-wife,' to use the word frequently found in conveyances and wills." – David Hackett Fischer, *Albion's Seed—Four British Folkways in America* [25]

Anthony₁ Gholson was named in a guardian's bond in 1744 as guardian to Hannah Durram, orphan of Robert Durram.[26] He had previously been summoned in 1729...

...to answer the presentment of the Grand Jury for keeping a bastard child unknown within this two months Last past, the Court having heard his Excuses and the said Anthony[1] having assumed to keep the said child of the Parish are of the opinion that the said Anthony[1] be Excused and accordingly order that yᵉ sd presentment be dismissed. – Brown & Altendahl, *Relatives of the Browns of Mill Springs, Kentucky* [27]

Anthony₂ Gholson reared two of his grandchildren after the death of their mother, Anthony₂'s daughter Kitty, wife of Bartholomew Hayden,[28] and he was also guardian for the two sons of Peter Evans for conducting a suit after their father died.[29] In spite of the high death rate, Virginians seemed to be relatively unconcerned about dying, in contrast with the Puritans in Massachusetts who seemed obsessed with the topic.[30] They did, however, make a great show of funeral ceremonies, often involving huge quantities of food and alcohol. Virginians were usually buried in a family plot, rather than a public burying ground as in the New England tradition.[31]

Social life
The opportunity for villagers to form bonds as they had in England was lost in America because the growing of tobacco quickly depleted the soil and colonists moved every few years.[32] However, the sense of community that was lost was transferred to the family and to neighbors within fifty miles or

so.[33] In 1624, the population of Virginia consisted of 1048 men and 244 women and children. Most of the men were single—called "adventurers" by the London Company.[34] When young Sir William Berkeley arrived in Virginia in 1642, the colony was a chaotic collection of roughly 8000 hard-drinking, uncivilized occupants. In Berkeley's thirty-five years as governor, the population grew to around 40,000 with a refined socio-economic system and "a governing elite which Berkeley described as 'men of as good families as any subjects in England.'"[35] It was before or during Berkeley's tenure that the parents or grandparents of *Anthony₁ Gholson* arrived in Virginia. *Anthony₁* was not among Virginia's elite, but he did acquire enough land to become a prosperous planter.[36]

Fig. 2.1 – Portrait of Sir William Berkeley. Courtesy of The Library of Virginia. POR-Berkley, Sir William, 1606-1677. Lab# 02-0389-01, CA9-430.

The uniform religion for the colony was the Church of England as promoted by seventeen laws passed in 1632 by the Virginia Assembly. Puritan and Quaker groups attempted to gain a foothold but were quickly squelched. By 1724 the Anglican church had very little competition and shaped the culture of the colony. In the late 1700's there was an increase of Presbyterians, Methodists and Baptists.[37] Shortly after moving to Kentucky in 1801, the grandson of *Anthony₁ Gholson*, whose name was also Anthony (referred to as *Anthony₂*), donated land for the construction of a Baptist church and cemetery, where he and his wife Elizabeth are buried.[38]

Speech patterns & literacy

Virginians developed an unusual way of speaking that did not resemble the speech of their New England contemporaries. Many common words were from old English expressions that were considered outdated in Britain, such as *bide* or *tarry* for stay, *botch* instead of blunder, *porely* or *pekid* for unwell and *favor* rather than resemble.[39] Many of these expressions are still commonly used by Virginians and their descendants in the southern states. The peculiarities of Virginia speech originated in seventeenth-century regional dialects spoken in the south and west of England. "The dialect of rural Sussex in the nineteenth century startled American travelers by its resemblence to Virginia speech."[40] In addition to retaining the old expressions for three centuries after they were considered archaic in England, Virginians added new words based on Indian and African expressions. The Virginians' speech pattern was soft and melodious, contrasted with the nasal whine of New Englanders. Dating back to the seventeenth century is the expression *you all* or *y'awl* in place of the plural *you*.[41]

The name of the county Botetourt was pronounced *Boat'a'tote* and for some unknown reason the name Crenshaw became *Granger*.[42] Also originating in England was the addition of the letter *y* between words, especially names, that ended and began with consonants, resulting in names like *Billy* and *Bobby*.[43] Many of the family names as they were pronounced bore little resemblance to the written version,[44] making it easy to understand why the name *Gholson* was spelled so many different ways, along with the fact that many people, including **Anthony₁ Gholson**, could not read or write even their own names.[45]

Literacy in 17th century Virginia among the elite was near one hundred percent but dropped to about fifty percent for the less wealthy male property owners, was lower among the laboring class, and almost nonexistent for women.[46] In the 18th century, the differences in the literacy rates increased between rich and poor, rather than decreasing, and the rich actively suppressed the education of the lower classes to keep it that way.[47] The ruling class deliberately restricted printing to keep reading material from the masses, while collecting impressive libraries of their own.[48] Governor Berkeley spoke for the Virginia elite in 1671 when he was asked about the state of education in Virginia:

> "I thank God," he declared, "there are no free schools nor printing, and I hope we shall not have these [for a] hundred years;

for learning has brought disobedience, and heresy, and sects into the world, and printing has divulged them, and libels against the best government. God keep us from both!"[49]

Although there was not an effort to educate the poor and help them to become rich, they were given help as needed. According to Thomas Jefferson in his *Notes on Virginia*,

> The poor who have neither property, friends, nor strength to labor, are boarded in the houses of good farmers, to whom a stipulated sum is annually paid. To those who are able to help themselves a little, or have friends from whom they derive some succors, inadequate however to their full maintenance, supplementary aids are given which enable them to live comfortably in their own houses, or in the houses of their friends. Vagabonds without visible property or vocation, are placed in work houses, where they are well clothed, fed, lodged and made to labor. Nearly the same method of providing for the poor prevails through all our States; and from Savannah to Portsmouth you will seldom meet a beggar.[50]

Sex, marriage & women's roles

Virginia had a definite patriarchal society, and marriage "was a social condition which everyone was expected to achieve. Bachelors and spinsters were condemned as unnatural and even dangerous to society."[51] In 17th century Virginia, so few immigrants were female that almost all women were able to marry, but there were only enough wives for about three-fourths of the men, and a man's ability to find a wife depended greatly upon his social status.[52]

There was a vast difference between Virginia and New England in sexual mores. In Virginia, pregnant brides and unwed mothers were common.[53] There were multiple rules applying to sexual behavior. While women were held to strict standards, men were encouraged and expected to engage in sex with any and all women, willing or not. In the diary of William Byrd II, he described his sexual adventures with "relatives, neighbors, casual acquaintances, strangers, prostitutes, the wives of his best friends, and servants both black and white, on whom he often forced himself, much against their wishes."[54] He always asked for God's forgiveness after the incident but continued to repeat the behavior again and again.[55] Rape, which was punishable by execution in Massachusetts, was punished lightly if at all in Virginia.[56]

Love was expected to follow marriage, not necessarily precede it. The recommended course was to take a wife that one could learn to love. Parents took an active role in deciding on a spouse for their children. Although children were seldom forced to marry against their will, they could be denied their inheritance if they did not comply with their parents' wishes. "Amongst landed families, marriage was regarded as a union of properties as well as persons, and the destinies of entire families were at stake."[57] Among the common people, women were responsible for the same household chores they had performed in England. Of necessity, they also became a partner in the fields, although deference to the man still remained. Women were not usually encouraged to read, write, or discuss political matters, as they were not considered intelligent enough, although there were exceptions in the upper class.[58] Thomas Jefferson wrote the following letter to his daughter Maria, while he was in New York in 1790:

> Where are you, my dear Maria? how do you do? how are you occupied? Write me a letter by the first post, and answer me all these questions. Tell me whether you see the sun rise every day? how many pages a day you read in Don Quixote? how far you are advanced in him? whether you repeat a grammar lesson every day? what else you read? how many hours a day you sew? whether you have an opportunity of continuing your music? whether you know how to make a pudding yet, to cut out a beefsteak, to sow spinach? or to set a hen? Be good, my dear, as I have always found you . . . [59]

Daughters of the top families in Virginia were instructed in running a household and supervising servants, as well as the social graces they would need to fill their role. Because the social life was so important, music, dancing and etiquette were essential skills for a young woman to acquire.[60] Although the slaves relieved southern women of most of the manual labor, great skill was required to maintain order, feed and care for them.[61] There were wooden floors to be sanded and polished, and every well-to-do family had large amounts of pewter and silver which needed frequent polishing. Huge collections of linen had to be maintained, without washing machines and steam irons.[62] Almost all food and clothing used by a family was grown and processed at home. Livestock was raised, slaughtered and cured, and grains were grown, threshed and made into flour. With the exception of a few items such as sugar and spices, all food originated with the family or a neighbor.[63] Candles and soap were made at home, in long and tedious processes, and even medicines were made by "the gathering and drying of herbs, the making of ointments and salve, the distilling of bitters, and the boiling of syrups. . ."[64] Some of the drudgery was relieved by turning work into social occasions, such as quilting bees, sewing bees, and many other "bees."[65]

The greatest burden placed upon the colonial woman was "the incessant bearing of offspring."[66] *Anthony₁ Gholson* and his wife, or wives, had at least five children;[67] his son *William* was the father of between seven and eleven;[68] and William's son, *Anthony₂*, was the father of eleven or twelve.[69] Children were an asset rather than a liability and more children meant more workers and the ability to generate more wealth for the family.[70]

Every member of an early Virginia family had a role to play, beginning at a very young age, and the welfare of the family depended upon every member. Planting, tending and harvesting crops consumed much of every member's time and energy. The day began and ended with prayers, and relatives who could not care for themselves were cared for and given whatever tasks they were able to carry out.[71]

It's a man's world

Virginia gentlemen were generally honest, hospitable and courteous toward each other, but in addition to their weaknesses of gambling and womanizing, many of them drank excessively. It was quite common to drink all day, from breakfast until bedtime, remaining in a "state of stupefaction"[72] except for those special occasions when they became exceedingly drunk. A Kentucky land transaction mentioned the old still house belonging to *Anthony₂ Gholson*[73] and he was undoubtedly following the example of his father in Virginia, as archaeologists have excavated stills in earlier Virginia compounds. The colonists distrusted water and had no coffee or tea until well past the mid-seventeenth century, but an early Virginian stumbled upon a way to make whiskey from corn mash.[74] They soon learned to make hard cider and peach brandy from the fruit of their orchards. "Regardless of laws passed...and sermons preached, excessive drinking remained common."[75]

As to recreation of Virginians, Robert Beverley observed, "They have Hunting, Fishing, and Fowling, with which they entertain themselves an hundred ways."[76] The various methods of hunting game included hunting hares on foot with dogs, hunting turkeys, trapping wolves, and hunting varmints such as raccoons and opossums with dogs by moonlight. The dogs would chase the game up a tree by the time the hunters caught up with them, "and then they detach a nimble Fellow up after it, who must have a scuffle with the Beast, before he can throw it down to the Dogs; and then the Sport increases, to see the Vermine encounter those little Currs."[77] Because of the danger of encountering larger animals such as bears and panthers, they also took the larger dogs along at night. Beverley also described the many methods of fishing and bird hunting.[78] **Anthony₂ Gholson's** family members were no exception and were described as "elegant people and wouldn't work, but loved to hunt."[79]

Nighttime

Night time posed a special set of problems and fears for early Virginians and the rest of the world before the invention of electricity. Roger Ekirch, Virginia Tech historian, has studied the preindustrial night for many years and shared his knowledge with Joyce and Richard Wolkomir in a *Smithsonian* magazine interview in the January 2001 issue. In prior centuries, "people relied on torches, hearth fires, smoking candles, walnut oil"[80] although only the rich could afford candles, and "for our ancestors, night meant fear of demons, witches and nighthags."[81] The difference between day and night was profound and although night provided anonymity for criminals and carousing gentry, many people in a variety of jobs worked at night, including bakers and dyers as well as those who performed offensive jobs such as emptying cesspools and collecting garbage. Methods of combating the darkness included wearing light-colored clothing or riding a white horse, but accidents happened frequently, especially when alcohol was involved. "People fell into ditches, ponds and rivers and off bridges; they were thrown by horses unfamiliar with dark paths."[82]

> People began as children to memorize their local terrain—ditches, fences, cisterns, bogs. They also memorized the magical terrain, spots where ghosts and other nighttime frights lurked. "In some places, you never whistled at night, because that invited the devil," says Ekirch. "You might wear charms or amulets around your neck, and nail horseshoes to your home to fend off witches."[83] – Joyce and Richard Wolkomir

Sleeping patterns were also different. Instead of sleeping from dusk until dawn, people slept in segments, awaking after four hours or so, lying in bed and meditating or even visiting with neighbors for one to three hours, then going back to sleep for another four hours. "People, as a matter of course, routinely referred to their 'first sleep' and their 'second sleep.'"[84] Beds were often the most valuable piece of furniture in the house, and it was common for an entire family to sleep in the same bed, often joined by visiting relatives or other travelers.[85] When *Anthony₁ Gholson* gave his property to his children before he died, two of his sons, **William** and **Anthony, Jr.**, each received "one Feather Bed & its Furniture."[86]

Social life & community activities

Eighteenth-century Virginians were inordinately fond of horses and were said to be "foaled, not born."[87] It was fortunate that they loved horses, as riding was necessary to get from one place to another.[88] Those who could afford it had expensive horses and handsome carriages, but even the poorest Virginian had a saddlehorse to ride. Walking was avoided like the plague, except when incidental to hunting. According to J.F.D. Smyth's observations of Virginians, recorded in 1772 in *A Tour in the United States of America*, "a man will frequently go five miles to catch a horse, to ride only one mile upon afterwards."[89]

The number one sport in eighteenth-century Virginia was horse racing, on which large sums of money were wagered. Fine horses were imported and carefully bred to bring out the most excellent qualities. It was during this period that the quarter horse was developed for great speed over a distance of a quarter of a mile in southern Virginia and North Carolina.[90] Not only did the Virginians bet on horse racing, but on card games, crops, the weather, and the like, with bets being enforced as contracts by the courts.[91]

In managing a plantation, the planter would oversee every detail, but if he owned slaves, it was the slaves who did all of the work, planting tobacco on the good soil and corn on the inferior soil. The best land was found under hardwood forests, so the trees were girdled to kill them and tobacco was planted between the stumps. Tobacco was grown for about three years, then the land was planted in wheat for a year or two before allowing it to revert to the forest, so planters had to continually move their plantations.[92] Jefferson predicted that when tobacco production declined, it would be replaced by cotton in the eastern parts of the state, and hemp and flax in the western parts.[93]

In 1784, a house was built for reception of deer skins and hemp, which were accepted as payment of taxes in Botetourt County, with *Anthony₂ Gholson* appointed as inspector. The post was an important one, because "much depended in those days on the quality of fiber secured, there being so many uses for it (rope etc.)."[94] The house was built on Thomas Madison's Stone House tract of land, and was described as follows:

> 18 x 24 feet, of round logs, 16 feet high, the lower story 10 feet,
> plank floors above and below, with a good door with sufficient

lock and key, covered with lapped shingles 18 inches to the weather clear of sap, the whole to be finished by the first of March in a workman like manner, for the reception of deer skins and hemp, agreeable to Act of Assembly. ***Anthony Gohlson*** was appointed inspector for the skins and hemp received, which were accepted as payment of taxes in the county. – *Kegley's Virginia Frontier* [95]

In a letter to John Adams, written at Monticello in 1812, Thomas Jefferson states, "We consider a sheep for every person in the family as sufficient to clothe it, in addition to the cotton, hemp and flax which we raise ourselves. For fine stuff we shall depend on your northern manufactories."[96]

The Virginia planters and their families were great socializers, often dressing in their finest clothing and going to join neighbors for elegant dinners and dancing, singing, card playing, drinking and holding philosophical discussions. The dances included minuets, reels and country dances, with music provided by French horns and violins.[97] The ability to dance was taken very seriously, and children were forced to learn to dance as a form of discipline, in contrast with the Quaker and Puritan colonies, where it was discouraged or forbidden.[98]

When it came to food, prosperous Virginians retained their English tastes, eating roast beef and fresh fruits and vegetables at every opportunity. The less prosperous often ate a "mess" of greens and salt meat or a bowl of hominy. Characteristics of Virginia cooking were roasting, simmering or frying, and highly seasoned dishes. For all social classes, feasting was an important ritual, taking place any time significant events occurred--weddings, christenings, holidays, or deaths.[99]

Child rearing

Although Virginians seemed indulgent in rearing their children, compared with the New England colonists, they instructed them very well in "formal rules of right conduct."[100] All children of all social categories were forced to learn them, but more rules applied to children from the higher ranks.

Among the earliest writings by George Washington was a list of 110 "rules of civility and decent behaviour in Company and conversation," which the young scholar had been compelled to inscribe in his best copybook hand:

1st   Every action done in Company ought to be with some sign of respect to those that are present...

19th   Let your countenance be pleasant but in serious
         matters somewhat grave...
26th   In pulling off your Hat to Persons of Distinction, as
         Noblemen, Justices, Churchmen &c make a reverence,
         bowing more or less to the custom of the better bred...
         - Fischer, *Albion's Seed* [101]

In the families of the American colonists, "Youngsters were taught... that what they did reflected first on the family, then rippled out to affect the entire community."[102] Children were given chores and responsibilities as early as three years of age and often had very little supervision during the day. "John Adams was given a gun when only eight, just old enough to lift it, and alone, under no watchful adult eye, he spent hours, day after day, in the marshes bringing down birds, or trying to."[103] There was no generation gap, as fathers and mothers worked with sons and daughters on a daily basis to teach them the things necessary to know to sustain life. Some children did not fare as well, as they were apprenticed out at an early age because the parents were unable to take care of them for one reason or another.[104]

Racial attitudes

There was a great difference in the attitude of Virginians toward Indians and Negroes. They saw Indians as noble savages with the capability of being transformed into civilized citizens, even though the Indians had no desire to become civilized.[105] The beginning of the end of friendly relations between the settlers and the Indians came in 1622 when Indians in Virginia suddenly and without warning killed 347 settlers across a hundred-mile area, followed by another attack in 1644, which gave the settlers an excuse to exterminate them.[106]

Much has been written which holds that after the first third of the century white settlers carried out a conscious criminal conspiracy to exterminate the Indian and that America ever since has been forced to bear a burden of guilt for what the past did to an innocent people. There is another view. "The American aborigine was the victim of a process," Bernard W. Sheehan has written in a perceptive essay on Indian-white relations in early America. "The crime, if there was one, was the inexorable breakdown of the native's cultural integrity, in part the result of conscious policy and in part the inevitable consequence of competition between two disparate ways of life."

Sheehan's judgment echoes that of Robert Beverley, who in 1705 published the first sympathetic study of Indian culture. Beverley ended his lengthy account about the way of life among Chesapeake Indians—"their dress...management of children...cookery and food...war and peace... concerning religion...diseases and cures...handicrafts"—with words that are hard to improve on nearly three centuries later:

> They have on several accounts reason to lament the arrival of the Europeans, by whose means they seem to have lost their felicity as well as their innocence. The English have taken away great part of their country and consequently made everything less plenty amongst them. They have introduced drunkenness and luxury amongst them, which have multiplied their wants and put them up to desiring a thousand things they never dreamt of before.[107]

The "noble savage" idea did not extend to Negroes, as shown by the following quote from *Undaunted Courage* by Stephen E. Ambrose:

> When they looked at a Negro, they saw something less than a human, something more than an animal. Never in their lives did they imagine the possibility of a black man's becoming a full citizen. William Clark tried to adopt a part-Indian boy as his own son. He would not have dreamed of adopting a black boy as his own son.[108]

In the early days of settlement, there were many more blacks in the North than in the South, but they were treated much like any other indentured servant. Slavery grew slowly in the South during most of the seventeenth century, partly because most slavers did not stop there, bypassing Virginia for more lucrative markets in the West Indies and Brazil. It was also less of a financial risk for a planter to buy an indentured servant for a few years than to buy a slave, due to the high death rate.[109]

Not all blacks in early seventeenth-century Virginia were slaves. Some were indentured servants, and some could even purchase white servants and testify against whites in court. There was even some tolerance for interracial marriage. Then beginning around 1660, Virginia and Maryland began passing laws banning interracial marriages and forbidding blacks to own property. They also forbade blacks to bear arms or travel without written permission.[110] Around 1670, several factors caused an increase in the number of slaves, including the following:

- There was a greater chance that they would live a longer life, making the investment less risky;
- The slavers began to tap into a market that had been ignored; and
- The role of the black man in society had deteriorated over the previous fifty years, making it more difficult for a black man to live free.[111]

New England-Virginia comparisons

Although in the beginning there were many similarities between the early colonies of New England and Virginia, it did not take long for them to develop their own distinct cultures. New England continued to maintain a rigorous religious focus with attention turning to commerce and trade.[112] The second and third generation Virginians, on the other hand, lived the aristocratic life on the plantations they had inherited and the social skills and knowledge obtained by being educated in England.[113] They became somewhat lazy due to the warm climate and ease of growing crops, preferring to hunt and socialize, rather than work, and the *Gholsons* were no exception. However, even though they admired and emulated English society, the Virginia aristocrats would prove themselves to be quite capable of rebelling against British authority when the time came.[114]

Three: Virginia – The Planters and the Land

Anthony₁ received a 1000-acre grant from King George II in 1728.
His son William received a 500-acre grant at the same time,
and he married Susannah Collins in 1725.
Their son Anthony₂ was born in 1733.
William's father, Anthony₁, died between Aug 1763-Dec 1764.

Private Property Rights

The right of property to an Englishman, native or colonial, was the primary and essential right on which all others rested. Attacks on property in the form of illegal levies or taxes had been the characteristic aggression of autocratic rulers.[1]

The fact is that..."power always follows property. Men in general, in every society, who are wholly destitute of property, are also too little acquainted with public affairs to form a right judgment, and too dependent upon other men to have a will of their own...Such is the frailty of the human heart, that very few men who have no property have any judgment of their own. They talk and vote as they are directed by some man of property, who has attached their minds to his interest." They were not, therefore, "independent men"—that magic status on which true republics must rest, men who owned property and thus could call their souls their own.[2]

Property...was the basic liberty, because until a man was secure in his property, until it was protected from arbitrary seizure, life and liberty could mean little.[3]
John Adams, Vol. I, by Page Smith

The possibility of acquiring land was a dream that attracted thousands of Europeans to the colonies. In Europe it had become almost impossible to acquire land that was not already in the family, but in America an abundance of land awaited anyone who wanted it.[4]

Private land ownership was dear to the Englishmen but was foreign to the Indians. The Indian considered all creation common property equally accessible to all and for the benefit of all. To the Indian, whose very existance [*sic*] depended upon his ability to hunt, fish and plant a small number of crops, the free use of the land was essential. The right to the land upon which the English chose to settle was claimed by the Powhatan Confederation. The English, on the other hand, did not recognize any sovereign right to the land or the use thereof in the Indian but rather claimed title and exclusive right to possession and use of the land under the generally accepted (in Europe) doctrine of title by discovery and later under the prevailing doctrine of effective occupation.

Though some land was purchased from the Indians and some was given to the English by the Indians, it is generally conceded that most of the land acquired by the English in Tidewater Virginia was taken from the Indians without benefit of either purchase or gift. It was seized by conquest, eviction and appropriation and the Indian was denied further access to it.

The Virginia Company of London or the London Company, and later the English Crown, recognized the problem and many attempts were made to protect the rights of the Indians, all to no avail. As the flow of settlers increased and the demand for tobacco land grew, there was very little desire or willingness on the part of the new residents of Virginia to recognize that the previous inhabitants had any rights at all to the land.[5] – Ulysses P. Joiner, Jr., *Orange County Land Patents*

Virginia was converted into a Royal Colony in 1624.[6] For each person transported to Virginia, the London Company assigned the rights to fifty acres of land, called "headrights," to the person who paid for their transportation.[7] Any freeman who paid his own passage received fifty acres for himself and for each member of his household.[8]

Virginia's Royal Governor Spotswood envisioned creating an English nation in North America as he led his party out of Williamsburg in 1716 to claim the Appalachian mountains for England and to stop the advance of the French in the interior. He and his party, whom he called the Knights of the Golden Horseshoe, climbed to the top of the Blue Ridge range on September 5, 1716, and looked down into the great valley and across to the Allegheny mountains. Then they descended to the Shenandoah River (named by the Indians and meaning *Daughter of the Stars*) where they buried a bottle containing Virginia's claim to the land for King George I.[9] For the next century, the American frontier was pushed back by ***Anthony₁ Gholson*** and his descendants and thousands of others like them.

Map 1

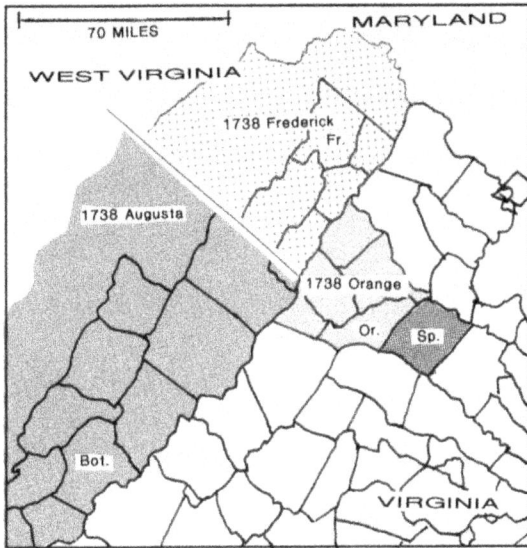

Current north central Virginia Counties showing
area covered by the following counties in 1738:

Augusta
Frederick
Orange
Spotsylvania

Map drawn by D. Cook. Copyright 2003.

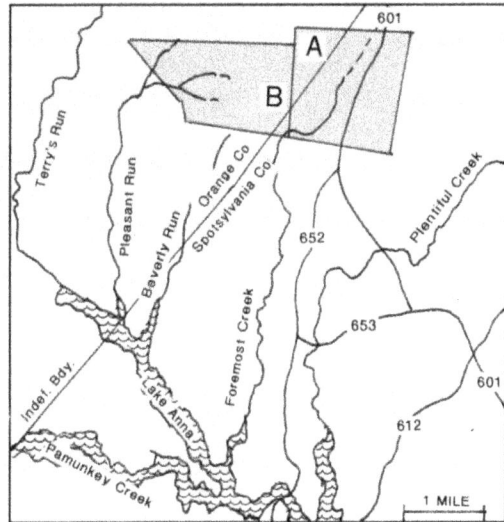

Map 2

Virginia Land Grants, 8 September 1728, then
Spotsylvania County, now Orange/Spotsylvania,
Courtesy of the Library of Virginia.
A. Anthony₁ Gholson, 1000 acres,
   Patent No. 13, 1725-1730, pp. 441-442
B. William Gholson and Anthony Gholson, Jr.
   1000 acres, Patent No. 13, 1725-30, pp 382-3.
Land grant outlines obtained from *Orange
County Land Patents*, 2nd Edition, by Joyner.
Topography from USGS 7.5 minute quads Lahore
and Belmont, photorevised 1973 and 1983, resp.
Map compiled by author. Copyright 2003.

~

The first Anthony Gholson in America
c. 1685-1764

It is not certain how many generations of Gholsons had been in America
before *Anthony₁ Gholson* was born sometime around the year 1685. His first
recorded transaction was a purchase of 200 acres of land for fifty pounds of
tobacco in Spotsylvania County, St. George Parish, in 1725,[10] which he and
his wife *Jane* sold in 1739 to Zachary Lewis.[11] In 1728 he obtained a grant
from King George II for 1000 acres on Terry's Run in Spotsylvania County.[12]
By 1738, he had sold all of the 1000 acres.[13] His sons *William* and *Anthony,
Jr.* received grants of 500 acres each at the same time he received the 1000
acres.[14] *Anthony₁* bought 400 acres in 1740 from John Chew and wife, and
sold 120 acres in 1744 and the remaining 280 acres in 1761.[15]

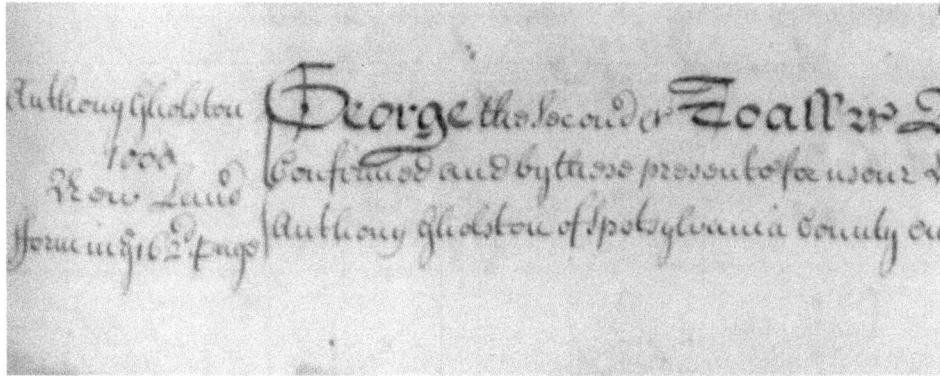

Fig. 3.1 – Sample corner of land grant to Anthony Gholston for 1000 acres by King George II. State Records, Land Office (RG4) Register of the Land Office, Original Patents and Grants 1728-1933, Patent Book 13: 1725-1730 [Microfilm Reel 12] 1000 acre grant to Anthony Gholson, 28 September 1728, pp 441-2 (copied in their entirety in Appendix 1). Archives Research Services, The Library of Virginia, Richmond, VA.

Most of those who settled in Virginia during the first hundred years had not moved beyond the fall line of the main rivers so that they could easily transport their tobacco to ships bound for England.[16] As the soil in that area began to be depleted from tobacco growing, landowners began acquiring new lands in the Piedmont and Valley sections of Virginia.[17] Moving inland from the water courses necessitated the building of roads to move the tobacco to seaports. When road building began, it became a function of the county courts to build and maintain the roads.[18] The following description of the road system is taken from Thomas Jefferson's *Notes on Virginia*:

> The roads are under the government of the county courts, subject to be controlled by the general court. They order new roads to be opened wherever they think them necessary. The inhabitants of the county are by them laid off into precincts, to each of which they allot a convenient portion of the public roads to be kept in repair. Such bridges as may be built without the assistance of artificers, they are to build. If the stream be such as to require a bridge of regular workmanship, the court employs workmen to build it, at the expense of the whole county. If it be too great for the county, application is made to the general assembly, who authorize individuals to build it, and to take a fixed toll from all passengers, or give sanction to such other proposition as to them appears reasonable.[19]

There are several references to *Anthony₁ Gholson* as caretaker and overseer of the road between 1727 and 1733 in Spotsylvania County. On August 1, 1727, *Anthony₁* was appointed to serve as overseer of the highways,[20] then he petitioned for more hands to be added to his road gang but the petition was rejected.[21] On February 5, 1729/30, he petitioned for discharge as overseer and his petition was granted.[22] On April 7, 1730, he was ordered to help Thomas Pulliam, who had been appointed overseer, as his replacement.[23] On November 6, 1733, *Anthony₁* was ordered to help Joseph Thomas to keep the road clear.[24]

The wealthiest Virginians owned as many as several hundred thousand acres of land, often split into many tracts. Robert Carter of Lancaster County owned approximately 333,000 acres.[25] *Anthony₁ Gholson* was not one of the wealthiest, but he was a prominent member of the community in Spotsylvania County and engaged in a number of legal transactions between the time of the 1000-acre grant and his death in his late seventies sometime before December 1764.[26]

On July 23, 1763, not long before he died, *Anthony₁* executed a deed of gift in Orange County, Virginia, to four of his five children, as follows:

- To son *William*, slaves named Tom and Little Tom, and one feather bed and its furniture;
- To son *Anthony, Jr.*, slaves named Bob and Cupid, and one feather bed and its furniture;
- To daughter *Elizabeth Rice*, female slaves named Venus and Mary;
- To daughter *Lucy Step [Stapp]*, female slaves named Phillis and Greece [or Creece], which he loaned to her during her natural life, with the slaves and their future children going to Lucy's children after her death; and one feather bed and its furniture; and
- To his granddaughter, *Jane Pollard*, female slave named Sarah.[27]

The above deed of gift reserved the use of the slaves and furniture to *Anthony₁'s* widow, *Jane Gholson*, for her lifetime. On August 8, 1763, *Anthony₁* executed a deed of gift to his son *John* for one lot of land purchased from Nathaniel Geer, the slaves Judy and Ben, all of his stock of horses and cattle, and all of the remainder of his estate.[28] *Jane* then executed a Deed of Gift on December 3, 1764, giving all of the slaves named above to her son *John*, for her lifetime, then they would revert to her other children as stipulated by her deceased husband, *Anthony₁*.[29]

William Gholson, son of Anthony₁ and Jane
c. 1705-1800

Anthony₁ Gholson's eldest son *William* was born around 1705 in Spotsylvania County. His first recorded transaction was the 1000-acre grant received jointly with his brother, *Anthony, Jr.* in 1728. He owned many slaves and many tracts of land in Spotsylvania County and Orange County, in the foothills of the Blue Ridge mountains in Virginia's Piedmont section, with his name appearing frequently in record books between 1747-1774. Even though *William* bought and sold numerous tracts of land, no record has been found of the settlement of his estate. He was married twice. His first wife was Captain Joseph Collins' daughter *Susannah Collins*, who died between 1775 and 1786. His second wife's name was *Joan*, but the names of her parents are unknown.[30]

William and *Susannah* had at least seven children, possibly as many as eleven.[31] Their first son may have been *Lewis Gholson* of South Carolina. The other children were *Anthony₂*, who moved to Kentucky in 1801, *Frederick, John, Francis, James,* and *William, Jr.*, and possibly one or more additional children.[32] *William* may have lived with his son *William, Jr.* until he died. It does not seem likely that he crossed the mountains into Kentucky with his son *Anthony₂* in 1801, as he would have been well into his nineties at the time.[33] *William*, like his father *Anthony₁*, signed his name with a distinctive mark, *Anthony₁* using a large capital "A" and *William* using an "M" with a slash through it.[34]

Anthony₂ Gholson
Son of William Gholson & Susannah Collins Gholson
c. 1733-1815

William's son *Anthony₂*, named after his grandfather, was born around 1733 in Spotsylvania County. *Anthony₂* married *Elizabeth Sandidge* in Spotsylvania County and they had twelve children during the years 1760-1786, *Francis, William, Mary (Mollie), Sarah (Sally), Elizabeth (Betty), Samuel, John, James, Benjamin, Nancy, Catherine (Kitty),* and *Dorothy (Dolly)* who married Micah Taul, whose life is described in Chapter 6.[35]

Anthony₂ rented a 113-acre parcel of land from George Washington in Frederick County above Worthington's Marsh from 1768 until 1786 or later and became delinquent in his rental payments. The following excerpt is from a letter written by George Washington to his brother Samuel Washington on December 6, 1771, discussing the best way to collect *Gholson's* rent:

You wrote me word sometime ago that a Tenant of mine, was desirous of raising money in your hands for the discharge of his Rent; if you think there is a probability of his doing of it, I should much rather take it in that way, than by distress, & should be glad if you would order it so accordingly, & ask the other's [*sic*], as you may accidentally see them, in what manner they purpose to pay; as I am resolvd, so soon as *Gholson's* Rent for the present year becomes due, to destrain for the whole; as I also will for all the Arrearages of Kennedy's after March when I think by his Lease I have a right so to do.[5] ...

... 5. *Anthony[2]* Gholson rented a 113-acre parcel of GW's Frederick County land above Worthington's Marsh from 1768 until at least as late as 1786. Rental was set at £4 a year. *Gholson* did not make his first payment until 19 Oct. 1772, at which time he paid £18.15.0 to cover his arrears through 1771 (Ledger A, 305; Ledger B, 31; *Frederick County Deed Book*, 22 Mar. 1769, pp. 10-12).[36]

In 1775, *Anthony[2]* apparently lived in Berkeley County, now West Virginia, which adjoins Frederick County, Virginia. He signed a Petition of Freeholders of Berkeley County to the "Honourable the Moderator and the Delegates of the Colony of Virginia in Convention assembled"[37] protesting an election in Berkeley County. The nature of the protest can be found in the following excerpt from the petition:

That Colo. Adam Stephen without consulting any person in the County as far as your Petitioners have been able to learn arrogated to himself the sole power of appointing the time of Election and notifying it to the public. That the time fixed upon by him for the election succeeded so quickly to the Notification and the Notification was given in so partial and private a manner that a great number of Freeholders did not hear of the election until it was over and many of those who did attend were not acquainted with it till the very day of the election.[38]

On July 27, 1775, the Convention declared the election irregular and ordered a new one.[39]

Some of *Anthony[2]'s* moves in Virginia can be traced by records from Augusta and Botetourt counties. (Botetourt County was created in 1770 from part of Augusta County.) In 1778, *Anthony₂* lived in Beverley Manor, Augusta County, where he bought 374 acres, which he sold in 1779.[40] He was a member of Captain Tate's Augusta County militia during the Revolutionary War.[41] Then in 1779, the names of delinquent taxpayers returned by the deputy sheriff for Augusta County listed "*Anthony[2] Golston*, gone to Botetourt"[42] where he and his family lived in the Buffalo Creek Community on the Roanoke River.[43] The fact that *Anthony₂* had moved may account for the missed musters resulting in numerous court martial summons issued for him in the last half of 1779 and may explain why he was acquitted.[44]

There were many legal transactions involving *Anthony₂ Gholson* in Botetourt County, Virginia, between 1780 and 1801. In 1783 he served on a jury.[45] The largest tract purchased in Botetourt County was 680 acres from Reverend Caleb and Rosanna (Christian) Wallace in 1784. Rosanna's brother was Colonel William Christian of Botetourt County, who was married to *Anne Henry*, a sister of *Patrick Henry*. The population of the region was sparse, such that there were frequent interactions between seemingly ordinary people and others who have become legendary figures in history. In addition, "*Thomas Madison*, owner of some of the land adjoining that purchased by *Anthony₂ Gholson*, was a son of *John Madison*, a cousin of *President James Madison*. Thomas Madison was married to *Susannah Henry*, another of *Patrick Henry's* sisters."[46]

The Botetourt County Court minutes show that *Anthony₂* was appointed Surveyor of the Road on May 10, 1785.[47] The minutes for November 8, 1785, show that James Robertson was "appointed to allot the hands to work on the road under David May and *Anthony[2] Gholson*."[48] *Anthony₂* was the Surveyor of the road until the appointment of David Goods on September 9, 1788.[49] Then on February 16, 1792, *Anthony₂ Gholson* was appointed Overseer of the Road.[50]

In 1785, *Anthony₂* assembled about 1000 acres which he sold in 1790. Then between 1790 and 1800, he again assembled several tracts[51] into a plantation of 1,180 acres in Botetourt County's Buffalo Creek Community, which was called the "Big Spring Estate." He sold all of the tracts to Daniel Stoner in September 1801. The transactions prompted a comment from Rev. Caleb Wallace that the "rich men were buying up all the land getting it into their own hands."[52]

An important development in early America was the sawmill, which utilized the numerous fast-running streams for power to turn the abundant wood into lumber for export and for use at home.[53] Another type of mill, the grist mill, required a larger investment, because of the necessity to import the stones from Europe which were used to grind grain. When the stones reached a seaport, they had to be hauled to the site of the grist mill and assembled and dressed by an expert.[54] *Anthony₂ Gholson* built a new grist mill in 1793[55] and on January 14, 1794, he was given a permit to build another one on his land on Robinson's Creek.[56]

> Grist milling...was a highly specialized craft. The ideal miller combined the skills of carpenter, cooper, joiner, blacksmith, and mason. He needed to be able to judge with eye and hand the quality of the grain, its age, its moisture content, its temperature, and then determine the proper speed to rotate his stones for the particular batch in hand...
>
> Others in the community might have more prestige, but no one exceeded the miller in practical importance. His presence could mean the difference between a subsistence existence and prosperity. Without him all grain had to be ground by hand and few farmers could produce enough surplus flour by that process to send to market. Flour the miller shipped to port towns returned in the form of pots and pans, axes and hoes, bolts of calico. Some millers opened small stores to serve the neighborhood. Often a hamlet cropped up around the mill site as it slowly became the economic and social center of the area...the gristmill and to a lesser extent the sawmill, both powered by water, worked for the backcountry of early America as an "entering wedge of a slowly emerging market economy." Both served the isolated settler as a window on the world beyond the farm.[57]
>
> David Freeman Hawke, *Everyday Life in Early America*

Mass migration to Kentucky through Cumberland Gap

After the Revolution, there was a decline in the price of tobacco due to overproduction, and the profit margin dropped drastically,[58] prompting many Virginia families to move to western Virginia, Kentucky and south into the Carolinas and Tennessee.[59] "At the time of the great migration into the Shenandoah Valley, Botetourt County encompassed the area which is now several counties in Virginia, part of West Virginia, and the entire states of Kentucky, Ohio, and Illinois."[60]

In 1801, the hardy sixty-eight-year-old *Anthony₂ Gholson* crossed the mountains into Kentucky with his family, including married sons and daughters, and his slaves.[61] The thought of moving west had probably been on his mind since 1780 when he received a grant of land in Jefferson County, Kentucky (in Virginia until 1792) for 992 acres on Bayles Trace. "These entries were the location of lands issued for service, sometimes as early as the French & Indian Wars (1753 on) but usually for Rev. War."[62] In 1783, there is a 200-acre tract entered in his name in Fayette County, then in 1802 there is a 105-acre tract entered in Wayne County, and in 1807 an additional 220-acre tract.[63] On May 2, 1803, two years after *Anthony2* moved his family to Kentucky, President Thomas Jefferson signed a treaty to purchase the Louisiana Territory from Napoleon for $15,000,000, doubling America's territory and opening the land from the Mississippi River to the Rocky Mountains for expansion.[64]

Four: Virginians in the American Revolution

Anthony₂, Gholson, born in 1733, age 43 in 1776

"... the War for Independence was largely fought and won in the South."[1]

Virginia's role in the American Revolution was a complex one; often it was a dominant one. Her statesmen and soldiers were involved in nearly every phase of the political, social, and military upheaval which transformed a group of thirteen isolated English colonies into a unified and independent republic. A Virginian was the second commander in chief of the Continental armies...and later the first president of the new nation.

Other Virginians conquered the Old Northwest, fought and won at Stony Point, fought Indians on the Ohio and in Georgia, and stormed the citadel of Quebec. Virginians tasted defeat at Charleston and Camden, suffered hunger and disease at Morristown and Valley Forge, rotted in prison hulks, and died as captives in New York City. Cannon, muskets, and powder for the Continental forces were fabricated in Virginia. Enemy armies twice invaded her, and a major British force surrendered within her borders. The names of Washington, Jefferson, Madison, Monroe, Marshall, and Mason are still venerated; those of Woodford, Lawson, Scott, Weedon, and thousands of others are lost in obscurity. Nevertheless, the future president and the nameless private each shared a common experience, and each played his own unique and vital part.[2] *A Guide to Virginia Military Organizations in the American Revolution*

Resistance to British authority

By the end of the Seven Years War, England owned territory stretching from Canada to the Gulf of Mexico, and the decisions that were being made regarding these lands began to irritate the colonists, particularly those in the middle and southern colonies. Some of the colonists, including George Washington, were making plans to buy land from the Indians when England issued a proclamation forbidding them to buy and settle the lands. Washington and others ignored the ban.[3]

King George III decided that the colonies would pay for the protection they were receiving from the military along with a portion of the expenses of the British government. The first step was to strengthen the Molasses Act which imposed a duty on foreign imports, eliminating the colonists' means of making money with which to repay their creditors in England. This did not prove to be effective, so it was decided that a fee would be charged to stamp all legal documents in the colonies, and the Stamp Act was passed in 1765. This would not have presented a major problem, except that it riled the journalists by including a tax on newspapers. The journalists made an appeal to those who were willing and able to organize and lead the resistance—men such as Patrick Henry in Virginia and Samuel Adams in Massachusetts. There was no general objection to the Stamp Act in America, but it was greatly opposed by the English creditors, as it hindered the ability of the colonial merchants to pay back the money they had borrowed, "because the duty had to be paid in bullion already needed for meeting the adverse trade balance with England."[4]

The Stamp Act was repealed, but in 1767 a tax was levied on American imports of several items, including tea. Although this angered the colonists, it was still not a good enough reason to revolt. After the colonists boycotted English goods, the duty was dropped for all of the items except tea.[5] Just when the trouble appeared to be over, British troops in Boston fired on a group of civilians who were throwing snowballs at them on March 5, 1770, killing five, and the Boston Massacre added fuel to the revolutionary zeal of Samuel Adams and others. A communication network of seventy-five towns was established. "The Virginian agitators, led by the young Patrick Henry, created a standing committee of their Assembly to keep in touch with the other colonies, and a chain of such bodies was quickly formed. Thus the machinery of revolt was quietly and efficiently created."[6]

Colonial anti-British sentiment was finally galvanized by the English government's effort to rescue the East India Company from bankruptcy. The company was given the authority to ship tea to the colonies duty free, thus destroying the American importers and their distributors. The Patriots, as they had begun calling themselves, disguised themselves as Indians, boarded ships that carried the first duty-free tea into Boston Harbor and destroyed the tea by dumping it into the water.[7] As a result, the British Parliament assumed authority, suspending the Massachusetts assembly and closing the port, and ordered that troops be quartered in the other colonies to maintain order. Instead of isolating the resisters as Britain hoped, these actions brought them together. A congress held in Philadelphia in September 1774 drafted a document which requested that the English Parliament repeal thirteen acts which had been passed during the preceding decade, but the petition was rejected.[8] Americans switched from tea to coffee, thereafter considering it unpatriotic to drink tea.[9]

None of the colonial governors sent by the Crown were very well liked, but Lord Dunmore, Governor of Virginia, was disliked more than most. Dunmore and Patrick Henry had been engaged in a power struggle for some time, with the most recent confrontation arising from Henry's speech at the Second Virginia Convention. All of the leading Virginians were present at that convention on March 23, 1775, in Saint John's Church in Richmond, including Thomas Jefferson and George Washington. Since **Anthony₂ Gholson** had rented land from Washington and purchased land from Patrick Henry's sister-in-law, he was probably personally acquainted with them and may have even been in attendance. The meeting was not expected to do anything other than ratify the acts of the First Continental Congress and approve delegates to the Second. **Then Patrick Henry rose to speak.**[10]

Fig. 4.1 – *Patrick Henry*, photograph of a painting by George B. Matthews, 1857-1935, in the United States Capitol. Detroit Publishing Co. No. M 9855. Gift; State Historical Society of Colorado; 1949. Library of Congress No. LC-D416-9855.

Most of the planters had no intention of opposing the king and were shocked when Henry demanded that a militia be raised in Virginia. They were really hoping to settle their differences and restore their former relationship with the king. Fighting the powerful Crown was the last thing on their minds.[11] Henry could not be persuaded to sit down and shut up, and he went to the podium again. His words became known as one of the greatest speeches ever given:

> **Reconciliation? What reconciliation? We are infested with armies and fleets sent from England. A military presence with only one purpose—to force our submission.**
>
> **And what is our reply? More argument and petitions? Sir, we have been trying that for the last ten years. We have nothing but the same old arguments to present. We have already done enough petitions, remonstrations, protestations.**
>
> **There is no longer any room for hope. If we wish to be free—if we mean to preserve inviolate those inestimable privileges for which we have been so long contending . . . we must fight! I repeat it, sir, we must fight! An appeal to arms and to the God of Hosts, is all that is left us!**
>
> **They say we are weak. But when shall we be stronger? Next week, or next year? Shall we wait until there's an army stationed here, a guard at every door? No.**
>
> **We are not weak. We are invincible in the holy cause of liberty. Three million people invincible by any force which our enemy can send against us.**
>
> **There is no retreat, but in submission and slavery! Our chains are forged. Their clanking may be heard on the plains of Boston! The war is inevitable—and let it come! I repeat, sir, let it come!**
>
> **Gentlemen may cry, peace, peace—but there is no peace. The war is actually begun! The next gale that sweeps from the north, will bring to our ears the clash of resounding arms! Our brethren are already in the field! Why stand we here idle? What is it that gentlemen wish? What would they have? Is life so dear, or peace so sweet, as to be purchased at the price of chains, and slavery? Forbid it, Almighty God! I know not what course others may take; but as for me, give me liberty, or give me death![12]**

His words were enough to light a fire in any soul, but his actions during the speech gave his words an even greater impact:

He delivered those words with a kind of wild theatricality. According to one account, "an unearthly fire burned in his eye" and "the tendons of his neck stood out white and rigid like whipcords. His voice rose louder and louder, until the walls of the building, and all within them, seemed to shake and rock in its tremendous vibrations." When he spoke of chains and slavery, he "stood in the attitude of a condemned galley slave, loaded with fetters, awaiting his doom. His form was bowed, his wrists were crossed; his manacles were almost visible." But when he exclaimed, **"Give me liberty, or give me death!"** he flung his arms wide as though shattering his bonds and struck the left side of his chest with a clenched fist as though driving a dagger into his heart.[13]

Benson Bobrick, *Angel in the Whirlwind: The Triumph of the American Revolution*

After a moment of stunned silence, Patrick Henry received a standing ovation. The convention continued—the acts of the First Continental Congress were approved and delegates were chosen for the Second. The delegates included Peyton Randolph, George Washington, and Patrick Henry. Thomas Jefferson was chosen as an alternate for Randolph.[14] Before the convention ended, each county was asked to raise "at least one company of infantry and one troop of cavalry."[15]

Lord Dunmore had forbidden the gathering at the Second Virginia Convention and the sending of delegates to Philadelphia. Both orders were ignored, and even more worrisome to Dunmore was the forming and training of militias. The news about Lexington had not reached Virginia when Dunmore sent a group of British seamen to confiscate the twenty-one and a half barrels of gunpowder which belonged to Williamsburg and take them to a ship. His excuse was that he might need the gunpowder in case of a slave uprising, but the planters demanded it back for the same reason. Since there were 140,000 slaves in Virginia, outnumbering the whites two to one, this was not an unreasonable fear.[16] The conflict escalated, with a threat from the colonists to march on Williamsburg, followed by a threat from Dunmore that if they did, he would arm the slaves and burn the city. The troops dispersed, fearing that he would carry out his threat. Patrick Henry was not so easily intimidated and postponed his trip to the Second Continental Congress to gather a group of frontiersmen to march on Williamsburg.

Although he often liked to pretend to be an unlettered country rustic, Henry was hardly a frontiersman himself. His father was a judge of the Hanover County court, as well as a county surveyor and a colonel in the Virginia militia. And Henry himself had an excellent education--from his father, at home, and also from his uncle Patrick, who taught him Latin, Greek, and the Bible.

In later years, Henry was to be widely known for rarely reading anything, but in youth he consumed books by the dozen, especially history, from which he could snatch apt examples and quotations. People soon discovered that this adolescent with his red hair that early subsided into a fringe and his excitable blue eyes was also an eager talker and a debater. From earliest youth, Patrick Henry liked a good fight.[17]

Hallahan, *Day the American Revolution Began*

The Virginia militia

With French, Spanish and Dutch assistance, the Patriot militia began collecting powder and supplies at Concord, where the Massachusetts assembly had reconvened contrary to the orders of Parliament. General Thomas Gage, who was the British military governor of Massachusetts, planned to confiscate the ammunition and arrest Adams and Hancock. The colonists monitored the activities of the English soldiers, and when Gage assembled his troops, the colonists' military supplies were dispersed to other towns. Samuel Adams and John Hancock went to Lexington. *Paul Revere* was at his post in the North Church steeple on April 18, 1775, when he saw eight hundred of Gage's men marching down the Concord road in darkness. After signaling with lanterns, Paul mounted his horse and raced to Lexington to warn Adams and Hancock. By sunrise when the British troops arrived at Lexington, the local militia was in place on the village green. The British officer at the head of the column ordered the colonists to disperse, then the militia commander ordered his own troops to disperse, but a shot was fired, starting a battle in which a number of the militia members were killed. It was April 19, 1775, and the Revolutionary War had begun.[18]

On April 26, seven days after the battle at Lexington, the news reached George Washington who was at home on his plantation, Mount Vernon. He immediately left for the Second Continental Congress in Philadelphia, taking with him his impressive Virginia militia uniform. The uniform would leave no doubt in the minds of the delegates that Washington was ready for a fight.[19] On June 15, he was appointed general and commander in chief of the

Continental troops, to the dismay of John Hancock, who was expecting to be asked to accept the position.[20] Washington had the military experience and leadership skills, and being a southerner, he brought the union together, but he was modest and did not feel that he was the most qualified.[21]

Fig. 4.2 – *George Washington in the Uniform of a British Colonial Colonel,* 1772, by Charles Wilson Peale, Washington – Custis – Lee Collection, Washington and Lee University, Lexington, Virginia. This is the first of seven portraits painted during Washington's lifetime by Peale, and the only one of him before the Revolution.

Peyton Randolph, the speaker of Virginia's House of Burgesses, was traveling by coach on April 27 when an express rider gave him the news of the battle of Lexington. Randolph was a wealthy and well-educated planter and was the cousin of Thomas Jefferson. He had been the president of the

First and Second Continental Congresses and was chairman of the Virginia group which was a part of the colonial network organized to oppose British rule.[22]

Randolph and the other tidewater planters were fighting to stay in power in the House of Burgesses as Patrick Henry and the small farmers like *Anthony₂ Gholson* from western Virginia tried to gain control.[23] Henry had been elected to the House of Burgesses at twenty-nine, about the same time as the Stamp Act was enacted.[24] He introduced his seven resolves, stating that Parliament had no authority to impose taxes on Virginia and that Virginians did not have to obey orders of Parliament. The bill passed in a modified form, marking the shift of power from the tidewater planters to the counties in Western Virginia.[25]

On Friday, April 28, 1775, the news of Lexington reached Williamsburg, Virginia's capital.[26] This would have normally been an active time of the year, but Governor Dunmore had closed the House of Burgesses the previous year and still refused to allow it to open. When his servants brought him the news of Lexington, he was already preparing to leave to escape from Patrick Henry and his troops who were marching toward Williamsburg. Dunmore had confiscated Williamsburg's gunpowder supply and the colonists were incensed.[27] On the night the news of Lexington reached Williamsburg, Patrick Henry's troops were camped about sixteen miles from Williamsburg. Henry demanded that Dunmore return the gunpowder or pay for it. Dunmore gave Henry a draft for the cost of the gunpowder, and Henry prepared to travel to Philadelphia to attend the Second Continental Congress. Dunmore returned to his palace and declared Henry an outlaw.[28]

Life returned to a somewhat normal state, but in addition to the spring planting activities, the militia continued to grow and drill and march.[29] The Virginia militia was composed of all white males between sixteen and fifty who attended monthly and quarterly musters, often electing their own officers, and "those who reported to the rendezvous were usually untrained, unarmed, and uninterested."[30] However, young men formed a social bond and gained experience with muskets, enabling them to defend their communities if needed.[31]

In order to convince citizens to move to the American colonies, the English government had promised to guarantee all of the personal freedom and property rights to the colonists that they enjoyed in England, including the right of Protestants to keep and use weapons. These rights were restated in the charters of Virginia and other colonies. The English common law was adopted in its entirety, unless the situation made it impractical, and the colonists added their own laws as they became necessary.[32] A major emphasis of the colonial governments was to "ensure that the populace was well armed,"[33] however Catholics were considered as potential subversives and Indians and black slaves were generally excluded from owning firearms.[34]

Colonial law went another step beyond English law and required colonists to carry weapons. A Newport law of 1639 provided that "noe man shall go two miles from the Towne unarmed, eyther with Gunn or Sword; and that none shall come to any public Meeting without his weapon." Early Virginia laws required "that no man go or send abroad without a sufficient partie well armed," and "that men go not to worke in the ground without their arms (and a centinell upon them)." They even specified that "all men that are fittinge to beare armes, shall bring their pieces to the church uppon payne of every offence, if the mayster allow not thereof to pay 2 lb of tobacco."[35] – Joyce Lee Malcolm, *To Keep and Bear Arms, The Origins of an Anglo-American Right*

Thomas Jefferson wrote the following description of the militia in his *Notes on Virginia*:

Every able-bodied freeman, between the ages of sixteen and fifty, is enrolled in the militia. Those of every county are formed into companies, and these again into one or more battalions, according to the numbers in the county. They are commanded by colonels, and other subordinate officers, as in the regular service. In every county is a county-lieutenant, who commands the whole militia of his county, but ranks only as a colonel in the field. We have no general officers always existing. These are appointed occasionally, when an invasion or insurrection happens, and their commission determines with the occasion. The Governor is head of the military, as well as civil power. The law requires every militia-man to provide himself with the arms usual in the regular service. But this injunction was always indifferently complied with, and the arms they had, have been so frequently called for to arm the regulars, that in the lower parts of the country they are entirely disarmed. In the middle country a fourth or fifth part of them may have such firelocks as they had provided to destroy the noxious animals which infest their farms; and on the western side of the Blue Ridge they are generally armed with rifles.[36]

The colonists strongly believed in maintaining a militia for self defense but they had a fear of standing armies which had grown out of generations of prior experience. King George II died October 25, 1760, and soon after the beginning of the reign of George III, it began to appear that these fears were justified.[37] The militia acts gave the British Crown more power over the militia and the ability to place it under the regular army. Then the proceeds from import taxes were used for the upkeep of the army in the colonies.[38] By 1775, the militia had come to be considered unreliable by the Crown, and the colonists were not confident in the ability of the militia to protect them. By the early part of 1775, patriots had begun to organize a selected group of individuals they trusted into a smaller militia of "minute men."[39]

In May 1775, Lord Dunmore reconvened the House of Burgesses while Patrick Henry and the other radicals were occupied in Philadelphia. Peyton Randolph turned over his position as chairman of the Continental Congress to John Hancock and returned to Williamsburg to preside over the House of Burgesses. Lord North, representing the Crown, had offered conciliatory proposals, but the proposals were rejected and Thomas Jefferson wrote the official reply.[40] Dunmore responded by offering emancipation to the slaves, which eliminated any hope of reconciliation between England and Virginia.[41] Thomas Jefferson personally carried the document rejecting Lord North's proposal to Philadelphia.[42] In 1776, Jefferson was given the opportunity of a lifetime when he was asked to draft a document declaring America's independence from Great Britain. After heated debate, the Declaration of Independence was approved by Congress on July 4, 1776.[43]

Thomas Jefferson was governor of Virginia when it was invaded by British forces led by Benedict Arnold in the fall of 1780. In January 1781, the capital of Richmond was captured and burned by a second British invasion. The state government was moved to Charlottesville, but the state archives were lost, destroyed, or captured, and Jefferson's home at Monticello was also raided.

Interestingly, Jefferson was so eager to secure Virginia's claims to the Ohio country that he had tried to send part of the Virginia militia to the region a few months earlier. The militia units, however, had mutinied and refused to leave Virginia.[44]
Davis and Mintz, *Boisterous Sea of Liberty*

Anthony[2] Gholson's roles

Anthony[2] Gholson may have also served in the French and Indian Wars, as he received a grant of 992 acres in 1780, in Jefferson County, Kentucky, on Bayles Trace.[45] These grants were given for service in both the French and Indian and the Revolutionary Wars. He served as a private under Captain James Tate in the Augusta County militia during the Revolutionary War.[46] Augusta County had been formed in 1745 from Orange County, which was originally part of Spotsylvania County.[47] Captain Tate's company fought the British on March 15, 1781, at the battle of Guilford Court House in North Carolina, but *Anthony[2]* had moved to Botetourt County in 1779 and probably was not a participant. Numerous court martial summons were issued for *Anthony[2]* in the last half of 1779 for missing musters, but he was acquitted, possibly because he had moved from the county.[48] British General Cornwallis held the field and technically won the battle of Guilford Court House but "had lost 800 men, including many of his best officers—twice the casualties suffered on the American side."[49] Captain Tate was one of the Americans who lost his life in the battle.

~

From the DAR Patriot Index:
Anthony[2]: b c 1733 VA d a 1-20-1817 KY m Elizabeth --- Pvt VA[50]

Five: Over the Mountains to Kentucky

Anthony₂ Gholson, age 68, moved with his family to Kentucky in 1801

. . . to the frontier the American intellect owes its striking characteristics. That coarseness and strength combined with acuteness and inquisitiveness; that practical, inventive turn of mind, quick to find expedients; that masterful grasp of material things, lacking in the artistic but powerful to effect great ends; that restless, nervous energy; that dominant individualism, working for good and for evil, and withal that buoyancy and exuberance which comes with freedom--these are traits of the frontier, or traits called out elsewhere because of the existence of the frontier.[1] – *Frederick Jackson Turner*

Daniel Boone

Many hunters had already passed through Cumberland Gap on the way to the good hunting grounds in Kentucky when Daniel Boone and his friend John Finley and four others left Boone's cabin on May 1, 1769. Daniel knew that his wife Rebecca would get along with the vegetables from the garden and the game shot and trapped by his eleven-year-old son James, and he hoped to bring back a profitable collection of skins and furs.[2] "Dressed in coonskin cap, buckskin jumper, and leggings, Boone disappeared for weeks at a time into the dense Kentucky wilderness, always to return."[3]

Fig. 5.1 – *Daniel Boone.* Courtesy of the Library of Virginia. POR-Boone, Daniel, 1734-1820. LAB# 03-1574-01, A9-17407.

As Daniel and his party approached the Gap, they were surprised to find a settlement under construction, led by Joseph Martin of Virginia. This settlement would be the last stopping point on the way to Kentucky for many settlers for years to come. Boone and the others crossed the divide and continued through the gap with its fifteen-hundred-foot cliff on the right side and a lower and rounder hill on the left. They followed an old Indian trail down to a ford on the Cumberland River and continued until they eventually reached Red Lick Fork, where they made their camp.[4]

Fig. 5.2 – *Cumberland Gap*, steel engraving by S. V. Hunt after painting by Harry Fenn. Copyright by D. Appleton & Co. Illustration in *Picturesque America*. Library of Congress No. LC-USZ62-52628 DLC (b&w film copy neg.).

There was such an abundance of game that the hunters had no trouble gathering a collection of furs and skins, but then Boone and his brother-in-law John Stuart had a run-in with a group of Indians. The Indians took their furs, captured them, and held them for a week before they were able to escape. By the time they made it back to camp, the camp had been plundered and their hunting companions had started home, so they did the sensible thing and resumed hunting. They had been hunting for a few weeks when Daniel's brother named Squire and a friend came to look for them because of their long absence. As soon as the rescuers found out that they were safe, they joined in the hunt themselves. The four of them continued trapping for several months, but then Stuart was killed by Indians, the other two left, and Daniel was left on his own to explore the wilderness. Squire took a load of furs home, then came back and the two brothers spent the winter of 1770-1771 hunting, trapping and exploring in southern Kentucky.[5]

By the time Daniel and Squire started home in March 1771, they had a good collection of furs and Daniel had decided to bring his family to Kentucky as soon as possible. Before Daniel and Squire reached home, however, another group of Indians took their guns, horses, supplies and their furs. For two years of work, the only thing they had to show was the batch of furs previously brought home by Squire.[6]

Still undaunted by his desire to move, by September 1773, Daniel had convinced a few other families to move to Kentucky, so forty people left the Clinch River area and started west. Boone's family and some neighbors were in the leading group and Captain William Russell was leading the second group. Boone sent back his son James, who was then seventeen, to give Russell directions on combining the two parties for the dangerous part of the trip. With James were Russell's son Henry and six others, including two of Russell's slaves, Adam and Charles. The group was attacked by Indians and were killed, with the exception of the slave Adam and one of the others, both of whom managed to escape.[7]

After the settlers buried the dead, they discussed whether to continue on or go back. Only Boone wanted to go on, but he eventually gave in and returned with the others.[8] The months that followed would bring more Indian conflicts before Boone could return to Kentucky.[9]

Daniel's next opportunity came when Colonel Richard Henderson of North Carolina asked him to be his agent and adviser in negotiating the purchase of roughly 20,000,000 acres of land from the Cherokee. The land encompassed the area between the Cumberland River and the Kentucky River, south of the Ohio River, as well as lands drained by tributaries of the Cumberland River.[10] In addition, Henderson secured a wide strip of land to provide access to the purchased land. He then gave Daniel Boone the job of cutting a road to Kentucky.[11]

Daniel gathered an assortment of axmen, friends, neighbors and others, and they left Long Island (Kingsport, Tennessee) on March 10, 1775, to blaze a trail of two hundred miles. As they approached Cumberland Gap, they again encountered Captain Joseph Martin, rebuilding the settlement he had left shortly after Boone's first visit.[12]

The axmen continued on, cutting the path through the mountains. As they came through a gap in the last mountain range, they saw the plains of Kentucky, covered with blooming clover and huge flocks of turkeys and other game. They knew they had found paradise.[13] After two more days, they were camped fifteen miles from the place where they planned to build a settlement, when a band of Shawnee Indians attacked them just before dawn. Two members of the group died and Boone built a barricaded shelter on the spot to care for the remaining wounded member, who soon recovered enough to be moved to the intended settlement location on the Kentucky River.[14]

Colonel Henderson had not bothered to consult any government authorities before he undertook to make the treaty with the Cherokee. The treaty and his plans for relocating 500 settlers did not meet the approval of Virginia and North Carolina authorities, including Colonel George Washington.[15] Henderson was not about to be deterred and left Long Island on March 28, 1775, with a group of around thirty horsemen. He followed the newly blazed trail, arriving at Martin's Station two days later. By the time he left there, his group had increased to around forty to fifty.[16]

Henderson's party was near Cumberland Gap when he received the letter from Boone describing the Indian problems.[17] He continued on, even though they met many persons returning from Kentucky because of their fear of the Indians. On April 20, 1775, they arrived at Fort Boone. Henderson took command and began revising Boone's plans, but gave him some recognition by naming the new capital Boonesborough.[18] Then he asked to have the area, which he called Transylvania, admitted as the fourteenth colony. In 1776, Virginia and North Carolina persuaded the first Continental Congress to refuse and Henderson's dream died. Instead, Kentucky became the westernmost county of Virginia.[19]

Among the many who used the road cleared by Daniel Boone's party was Thomas Lincoln, Abraham's father.[20] The road remained the same until Isaac Shelby took office as governor of Kentucky, which became the fifteenth state of the union in 1792.[21] Shelby decided that the road needed to be improved.[22] With the limited funds that could be raised, Colonel John Logan and Colonel James Knox supervised crews in widening and shortening the road.[23]

Shelby's next step was to improve the mail service. The federal government had established the postal service in 1789, and Kentuckians demanded that it be extended to them, which was done in August 1792.[24] Attempts to establish a route either overland through Cumberland Gap or down the Ohio River both had unsatisfactory results. Finally, both routes were used, although the Ohio River was not navigable in the winter.[25]

By the end of his administration, Governor Shelby approved an act which called for major improvements. A good wagon road to Virginia was badly needed.[26] Daniel Boone, who was then sixty-two years old, poor and without land, wrote to the Governor to ask for the job.[27] Daniel had never been paid for the original job and hoped to earn the money for the rebuilding work. The governor, however, appointed Colonels James Knox and Joseph Crockett to make the improvements. The route cut by their surveyors seldom touched Boone's route, which was abandoned, and the new road became the Wilderness Road.[28]

To advertise the completion of the improved route, the following announcement was made in the *Kentucky Gazette* on October 15, 1796, and printers in other states were requested to publish the notice:

> THE WILDERNESS ROAD from Cumberland Gap to the settlements in Kentucky is now compleated. Waggons loaded with a ton weight, may pass with ease, with four good horses,-- Travellers will find no difficulty in procuring such necessaries as they stand in need of on the road; and the abundant crop now growing in Kentucky, will afford the emigrants a certainty of being supplied with every necessary of life on the most convenient terms.
>
> JOSEPH CROCKETT
JAMES KNOX
Commissioners[29]

~

Anthony₂ Gholson

In the fall of 1801, the year that President Thomas Jefferson was inaugurated, *Anthony₂ Gholson* at age sixty-eight crossed the mountains from Virginia to Kentucky with his family and as many as eighteen slaves.[30] In all likelihood, they travelled along the new and improved Wilderness Road. There were more than a hundred thousand people in Kentucky, with more coming every day.[31] A man named Moses Austin had come across the road in December 1796 who, like some of the **Gholsons**, would also wind up in Texas where he would establish the Austin colony with his son Stephen.[32]

When *Anthony₂ Gholson* and his family arrived in Kentucky in the fall of 1801, Wayne County had just been created, the first meeting of the county court having been held in March of that year. A log building was constructed for a courthouse and fifteen-year-old **Micah Taul** was appointed clerk of both courts, the county court and the court of quarter sessions.[33] Much of the court business in the early years was concerned with building and maintaining roads, which were vital to reach the mills that were located on the rivers.[34] The judicial system in Kentucky was changed in 1804-1805, abolishing the District and Quarter Sessions Courts, and replacing them with Circuit Courts.[35]

A tract of public land had been set aside for the town site.[36] Four families lived in the town at the time, the families of William and Joseph Beard, Roger Oatts, and Henry Garner. Joseph Beard was a merchant and his clerk was **Ben Gholson**, the young son of **Anthony₂**. The first trustees of the town were **Anthony₂ Gholson**, George Singleton, Roger Oatts, John Hammond, and Isaac Crabtree. The first constable was Joseph Wheeler. When a jail was eventually needed, Roger Oatts, tavern keeper, was designated as the first jailer and he used a log house adjacent to his tavern for the jail.[37]

Augusta Phillips Johnson described the birth of the town in *A Century of Wayne County, Kentucky*:

> It is county court day: then as now, the good citizens have assembled--a clerk is to be elected--the town is to be named. Some are gathered at the town spring, others are drinking, fighting, and pillaging "for fun." A squad of militia, commanded by Lieutenant Bill Jones, is drifting near the spot where the old jail stood. We can see in the crowd, *Joseph Chrisman*, William Cullom, *Anthony[2] Gholson*, Isaac West, *Bartholomew Hayden*, John Buster, Louis Coffey, Squire Baker, Thomas Eades, Solomon Dunagan, Leonard Dodson. These first settlers came mainly from West Virginia, North Carolina, and Tennessee.[38]

Joseph Chrisman, his brother *Isaac Chrisman*, *Bartholomew Hayden*, and *Micah Taul* each married daughters of *Anthony₂ Gholson*. Bartholomew's sister, *Mary "Polly" Hayden* married *Anthony₂'s* son *Benjamin*.[39]

When the town was named, there was some controversy over which name to choose. *Micah Taul* suggested calling the town Monticello, after Thomas Jefferson's home, but the Jones family who lived in the area wanted the town named after them. When Taul's suggestion was adopted by the court, the Jones family developed a grudge against him. Later Micah was elected to a post of military captain instead of William Jones, who had his eye on the position.[40] Jones became so enraged that he attempted to whip Micah, but as Micah described it, "His rage unmanned him and as luck would have it I whipped him, according to the fighting phrase of the day. After a hard fight, fist and skull, biting, gouging &c, I came off victorious."[41] It took years for Jones to get over the humiliation of being beaten by the much smaller Taul, but eventually, Jones and Micah became close friends.[42]

Anthony₂ Gholson built a large house for his family near Steubenville which was owned by the Bohon family for over one hundred years. The house, below and to the east of the Steubenville cemetery, was owned by the Al Landreth family from 1972 until 1977, when it was destroyed by fire. "A call was made to the Monticello Fire Department but due to the lack of a $100 guarantee as required, they failed to respond and the home was completely leveled."[43] The following description was written by Margaret Gray who was born in the house, a fourth generation descendant of the Bohon family, who would have had to have moved into the house in 1820, prior to the birth of John L. Bohon:

> It was a log house put together with mortar. It had six rooms and three porches. The road used to go in back of the house for quite awhile, then was closed off. There was a huge stone fireplace in the east end of the kitchen, which was closed up and the chimney torn down in the thirties. The rocks were used to make a fence at the old Correll front yard by the Stubenville [*sic*] cemetery. There was a huge room for a cellar under the house. You entered from a door in the floor of our dining room and went downstairs.[44]

During the Civil War Battle of Mill Springs, wounded soldiers were brought to the house, a part of which was used as a hospital.[45]

There are many references to *Anthony₂ Gholson* in the Wayne County, Kentucky deed books from 1801 until his death and through the administration of his estate. In deeds of gift executed August 18, 1813, *Anthony₂* gave away slaves and household furniture, which would seem to indicate that *Elizabeth* had died, although she was still alive in 1810.[46] In 1815, *Anthony₂* donated land for a Baptist church and cemetery at Steubenville, about ten miles northeast of Monticello.[47] The log church was built with wooden pegs and "was razed in the eighties [1880s] and a frame house built."[48] The wooden pegs were actually superior to metal nails, because while nails can rust away or split the wood, the wooden pegs breathed with weather changes and eventually welded into the wood.[49] *Anthony₂* died intestate at some time between September 26, 1815, and March 1816, and documents in Wayne County, Kentucky deed books show the disposition of estate, including legally transferring the property to the church, as the deed had not been recorded during his lifetime.[50] He was also one of the organizers of the Big Sinking Baptist Church in January 1804.[51] A tribute to him was written in the Bible of one of his descendants, stating that he "was a Baptist, an ardent supporter of the faith, and gave the ground for both the church and the burying-plot (wherein he lies in an unmarked grave) at Steubenville, where he spent his latter years."[52]

The Boone and Gholson families, along with countless others, are examples of the pioneers' advance across America. Daniel Boone's son explored the Rocky Mountains and he and his party "are said to have been the first to camp on the present site of Denver. His grandson, Col. A. J. Boone, of Colorado, was a power among the Indians of the Rocky Mountains . . ."[53]

As Americans moved westward, the first group were the pioneers, who depended upon native crops and hunting to survive. When they felt the urge to move on, the next class of emigrants moved in to introduce a bit more civilization in the form of roads, bridges and additional cultivated fields. Following them were the "men of capital and enterprise"[54] who created substantial buildings and towns. There were a few in the first two classes who remained behind to advance in society, but there were far more who often sold out and moved, perhaps only a few hundred miles. [55] The *Gholson* family was a good example of the movers. *Anthony₁ Gholson* and his son *William* moved gradually across Virginia, then *William's* son *Anthony₂* moved to Kentucky, and his son *Francis* moved to Illinois, son *James* moved to Tennessee, and sons *Samuel* and *Benjamin* moved to Texas.

Fig. 5.3 – Photos of Anthony Gholson home near Steubenville, Kentucky. Courtesy of the Monticello *Outlook* and the Wayne County Historical Society.

Six: Anthony$_2$ Gholson Family Connections

CAPTAIN JOSEPH COLLINS & SUSANNAH LEWIS

Anthony$_2$ Gholson's mother was *Susannah Collins*, daughter of *Captain Joseph Collins*, who fought in the French and Indian War (also known as the Seven Years' War), and *Susannah Lewis*, the daughter of *Zachary Lewis*. On November 6, 1750, Joseph Collins took the oath as Captain of a Troop of Horse. The troop was to join the Culpeper County Militia to fight the Indians above Winchester in 1756. He is also listed as a Captain of Company of Foot.[1] The French and Indian War (1754-1763) marked the turning point where Americans began to feel less dependent on the British and began to think of themselves as Americans and not British.[2]

Joseph Collins died in 1757, a reasonably wealthy man, and an inventory of his estate gives some insight as to how few possessions were owned, even by the wealthy, at that time. The list of items also tells us a lot about his life. His property, excluding land, was worth about £470, and £300 of the total was represented by the value of eight slaves:

> 1 negroe man Named Osea
> 1 negroe Woman Named Sooe
> 1 negroe Girl Named Indey
> 1 D° Named Phillis
> 1 D° Named Hannah
> 1 D° Named Winney
> 1 negro Boy Named Peter
> 1 D° Named Munk[3]

The following items comprise the remainder of the estate:

> 5 Head of horses
> 1 Cart & wheels
> 5 Feather Bedds & Furniture
> 1 Desk
> 2 Black Walnut Tables
> 1 Black Walnut Coubbard
> 1 large looking glass
> 1 Gunn
> 1 Hone 3/6 one Razor 1/3 one Strop 1/3
> 1 Mans Saddle

1 Pr. of Pistols & holsters
1 Large brass kettle
4 Iron Pots & three Pr. pothooks
2 Iron Pot Racks
16 head of Sheep
3 Wooling Wheels & one flax Do
1 Large Pine Table & one Small Do & one pr. of money scales
20 Head of Cattle
3 Chests
A parcel of Old Pewter with some Lumber
1 Silver hilted Sword
1 Old frying pan 1/3 one small Trunk 2/16
3 Iron wedges & old lumber Iron with it
1 Cross Cut Saw & old Jointer
1 Pr. of Hillards
1 Brass warming pan
a parcel of Chairs
a parcel of Corn about fifty Barrells
a Parcel of fine earthen ware
a Parcell of Coarse Ditto
1 Case of Bottles
1 Candle Stick & one nut meg greatter
a Parcel of old Books & 1 Brush
a Parcel of Butter pots and Bottles
3 Bells & one Curry Comb
2 Small Casks
1 Washing Tub & two pails
1 Pocket Ivory Case & some brass forks
1 Loom & Gears
To Some spun wool & Cotton
2 Slain Cowhides
1 Womans Saddle & Bridle
A Parcel of Tand Leather
A Parcel of Reap Hooks & one Smoothing Iron
40 head of Hoggs
One Hundred Gallon Cask & one Rundlett
1 Cask & Laundering Tub & one Chest[4]

~

MICAH TAUL

Fig. 6.1 – Portrait of Micah Taul. Courtesy of the Wayne County Historical Society.

   Micah Taul was one of the most fascinating characters associated with the family of *Anthony₂ Gholson* in Wayne County, Kentucky. *Micah* became the County Clerk of Wayne County just before he turned sixteen and married *Dorothy "Dolly" Gholson*, *Anthony₂'s* youngest daughter, when he was seventeen. At twenty-eight he was the youngest commissioned colonel in the State of Kentucky, commanding the 7th Regiment,[5] which included *Dorothy's* brother *Samuel Gholson*.[6]

   Micah Taul wrote his memoirs in 1848-1850, the last two years of his life, leaving an excellent record of his experiences in the early colonization of Kentucky, some of the major battles in the War of 1812, and an eyewitness account of the governing of America in the nation's formative years. In addition, his memoirs contain much information about the family of *Anthony₂ Gholson*, his father-in-law, whose life was undoubtedly as interesting as Micah's, if he had only written it down. A fairly accurate birthdate for *Anthony₂* can be assumed as 1733 because of Micah's description of *Anthony₂* as around eighty in 1813 when he rode ten or twelve miles from his home to meet and welcome Micah home from the War of 1812.[7]

Micah Taul was born in Maryland, just north of the city of Washington, on May 14, 1785, the youngest of six sons. His parents moved to Fayette County, Kentucky when Micah was two years old and Kentucky was a wilderness. Most of the education Micah received was from his brother Benjamin who was a school teacher.[8] He described Benjamin as "the very best man I ever knew"[9] and it was through Benjamin that he was given a job in a clerk's office at the age of thirteen.[10]

When Micah was about seven years old, he had his first experience with death when his brother Pentecost drowned in the Kentucky River.[11] His brother Jonathan was a farmer who died "by falling from a tree on the end of an axe handle."[12] Micah's brother Levi married Nancy Copher, whose mother was the daughter of George Boone, brother of Daniel Boone. Levi suffered for many years from what is described as a "hemorage of the lungs."[13] Micah's brother Samuel also had poor health, but was a good farmer and raised a large family with his wife, Polly. Micah described his brothers as being "remarkable for their morality and steady habits."[14] He wrote in his memoirs that "neither of them was ever intoxicated with spiritous liquor,"[15] which was quite unusual for that time and place with its population of "plain, honest, rough"[16] backwoodsmen.

Micah loved school and realized at an early age that he did not want to be a farmer. His handwriting was so good that at the age of thirteen, upon his brother Benjamin's recommendation, he went to work in the office of a Revolutionary War captain named David Bullock who was Clerk of the County Court of Clarke County.[17] While working for Bullock, Micah was very impressed with the court speeches of a young lawyer named *Henry Clay*, so impressed that he decided to pursue a career as a lawyer.[18] The young Micah worked diligently and advanced quickly in the office of Captain Bullock.[19]

Wayne County was established in the 1800-1801 legislative session from portions of the counties of Cumberland and Pulaski. Micah was the candidate for clerk of both the Quarter Session and County Court. He had the recommendations of Captain Bullock, the Quarter Session judges and many other prominent citizens.[20] There were many qualified candidates for the position, including the county surveyors for Pulaski and Cumberland counties. The first court day was March 16, 1801, drawing many residents of the new county to watch the proceedings. Six judges undertook the job of electing a clerk. Micah, having started with one vote in the voting process, eventually won five votes out of six. He was elected clerk of both courts two months before his sixteenth birthday.[21] He had passed an examination the previous October which established his qualification for the job, having answered every question correctly.[22] One of the Quarter Session Judges was *Colonel Isaac Chrisman*, whose wife *Sarah* was a daughter of *Anthony₂ Gholson* and the sister of Micah's future wife, *Dorothy*.[23]

The description of Micah's first encounter with *Dorothy* is taken directly from his memoirs, as follows:

> In the fall of the year [1801], Anthony[2] Gholson removed from Botetourt County, Virginia to Wayne County, Kentucky. He had previously purchased a valuable tract of land and plantation five miles N.E. of Monticello on the road to Pulaski. His son John and his youngest daughter, Dorothy, were one day ahead of the family, when they passed Isaac West's where I boarded. It was a cool, damp evening, the young lady was wrapped up in a large blue cloth cloak, her face veiled and an umbrella over her. I guessed that they were members of that family, and as they passed I remarked to my brother Jonathan, who was then with me, that "that young lady was to be my wife." I saw her a few weeks afterward at a wedding (Abel Shrewsberry to Miss Tabitha Van Hoagan) and soon became enamoured of her. On the 20th of May six days afterward I was 17 years old, we married with the approbation of both of our families.[24]

Micah acknowledged that at seventeen he was very young, and his wife was even younger, but he was doing a man's job. He began to study law, buy property, and build cabins. His father gave him a young male slave named Frank who remained with the family until he died in Alabama, and Dorothy's father *Anthony₂* gave her a young female slave named Agnes who was still with the family at the time the memoirs were written.[25] Micah and Dorothy's first son, Thomas Paine Taul, was born two months before Micah's eighteenth birthday.[26]

Thomas Jefferson's Louisiana Purchase was ratified in 1803 and Kentucky was called upon to furnish 5000 troops to take possession of the land if it was not surrendered. Micah raised a company in Wayne County with no difficulty, but the need to fight did not arise at that time.[27]

Micah and Dorothy's second son was born in October 1804 and they named him Algernon Sidney. A third son died a few days after he was born.[28] A daughter named Louisiana was born in March 1808.[29]

By that time, Micah was a lawyer. Between his farm, his clerk positions and his law practice, he had a good income. He said in his memoirs, "It was then fashionable among the profession to play cards, for money. . . . I seldom sat down to a card table without losing a great deal."[30] Later, gambling on cards became unfashionable and he quit.[31]

Micah's role in the War of 1812 led to his *election to Congress in 1814*, with the enthusiastic support of the men who had been in his regiment in the war. He was Clerk of the Circuit Court of Wayne County at the time and resigned the position, to which his nephew John Chrisman, who had been working in his office, was elected. In November 1815, Micah left Monticello for Washington on horseback, which was still the chief mode of travel at the time.[32] "The Capitol was at that time in ruins, and Congress sat in a house prepared for the purpose about 150 or 200 yards east of the Capitol."[33] Fellow Kentuckian *Henry Clay* was elected Speaker of the House and Micah was appointed to the Committee of Enrolled Bills. Micah described himself as a silent member but one who actively participated. The popularity of Micah and most of the rest of the Kentucky delegation sagged when they voted for an unpopular bill,[34] and he chose not to run again. He redeemed himself during the next session, however, by making a speech in favor of the repeal of the bill, even though he was no longer a member of congress.[35]

HENRY CLAY,
1095

Fig. 6.2 – Portrait of Henry Clay, statesman, 1777-1852. Lithograph by Charles Fenderich, 1805-1887. Library of Congress No. LC-USZ62-1095.

Micah was in the audience on the day James Monroe was sworn in as president "on a temporary platform erected in front of the house in which Congress had held its sessions."[36] He rode home the next day in the company of the senator from Tennessee, Colonel John Williams, and a representative from that state named Bennett Henderson who became the minister to Guatemala under John Adams. Micah returned home to practice law and placed his sons under the tutelage of Samuel Wilson, leaving one child at home, daughter Louisiana who later married General Bradford.[37]

During the summer Micah became dissatisfied with Wayne County and decided to move. After visiting several places in Alabama and Tennessee, he decided to move to Winchester in Clarke County, Kentucky, which turned out to be the second greatest mistake he ever made, by his own description, the worst being voting for the unpopular bill in congress. He chose the Winchester area because he was partly raised there and he was able to be near his brothers again. He quickly built up his law practice.[38] For several years he was "the most popular lawyer at the bar of Paris in Bourbon County, one of the most populous and wealthy counties in the state."[39] However, he made the mistake of becoming associated with a noted criminal attorney, whom he described as "a man of decided talent and commanding eloquence, but I always thought he had as much character as he deserved."[40] Together they won the acquittal of a defendant in a murder trial and a few years later they won acquittals in a trial of two men accused of beating an old man to death. The men were acquitted due to contradictions in the dying man's declaration, but the people were not pleased with the verdict and they hanged the judge, jurors and lawyers in effigy on the town square. When an influential resident of the county attempted to cut them down, he had to leave town to keep from being mobbed. One of the defendants left the state and the other was shot and killed a few weeks later.[41] No attempt was made to find and prosecute the killer.[42]

Micah won another controversial criminal case in the spring of 1819 or 1820 in which he said, "three men were charged with having committed an outrage on the person of a female in Wayne County, where I still continued to practice."[43] This was another case in which public sentiment ran high against the defendants. Several prominent citizens asked Micah not to defend them and told him that the three men were guilty without any doubt. "Two of the men were married men of respectable families and were on bail; the third was a widower of not more than ordinary standing in society, and had been committed to jail for want of bail."[44] In talking with the defendants, Micah became convinced that they were only guilty of poor judgment, and not the offense as charged, and he decided to defend them.[45]

The man in jail was the first to be tried. The judge made a great show of protecting the woman with armed guards as she went from the house where she was staying to the courthouse and back, where the judge and attorney general were also staying with the excuse of guarding her, but in reality were attempting to manipulate the public sentiment against the defendants.[46] Micah decided to do a little manipulating of his own. The judge was already disliked, and it was easy to create antagonism toward him as Micah mingled with the crowd. Through Micah's subtle efforts the people began to change their attitude toward the defendants. When the trial of the man in jail began and the woman was brought to the courthouse under guard, Micah "took the liberty of 'looking daggers' at the Judge and interchangeing indignant glances with others."[47] The woman was a believeable witness and Micah was beginning to have doubts as to whether he would be able to disprove her testimony. After the testimony was finished, a respectable man came to Micah and told him something that contradicted the witness on a material point. Until that moment the man had given the information to no one, because the public was so inflamed against the defendants that he feared for his safety.[48] One can only imagine what his information may have been, as Micah did not reveal the nature of it. After the new evidence was heard, the jury returned a verdict of "not guilty" and the local citizens realized that they had made a mistake in condemning the men. Micah's argument took two hours, during which the judge left the courtroom. The judge had become an enemy for life when Micah had beaten him in the congressional election in 1814.[49] In fact, the judge did not like anyone in Wayne County because when he ran for congress in 1812 and 1814 he had received only eighteen votes there.[50]

The other two defendants were tried and easily acquitted. Micah purposely avoids mentioning their names, but he said "One of them is a respectable man with a large family, residing at present in Texas—one was hung a few years ago, in Arkansas, for murder."[51] That defendant was Charles Cox, also known as Cocke.[52] There is little doubt that the one who moved to Texas was Micah's wife's brother Samuel, which would explain why Micah was willing to take the case in the first place and his reluctance to give the names of the defendants. According to Micah's memoirs,

> They got themselves involved in this great difficulty by
> dissapation; they had been the preceding day at a deer hunt, fish
> fry, etc., where they had indulged freely in drinking, as well as
> eating, they were 15 or 20 miles from home and started to go
> home after night but stopped at a "doggery" by the way side
> where they became involved as above.[53]

The possibility of Samuel being one of the defendants would also explain an excerpt from an 1898 letter published in *A Century of Wayne County, Kentucky*, which states, "Sam Gholson was very wild and did a great many naughty things and Ma says every time she asks the early settlers here about them, they tell her about Sam. They seem to remember him better than the rest."[54]

Not long after the case was finished, Micah made a trip to Missouri with the idea of possibly moving there. Some of his old friends were members of the legislature, including Bennette Clark, brother of George Clark of Kentucky, and Colonel Jesse Boone, the son of Colonel Daniel Boone. Daniel died that winter and the legislature adjourned to honor his memory.[55]

Micah decided not to move to Missouri, although he felt that he would have done well there. He visited Tuscaloosa, Alabama in 1821 but was not impressed.[56] He lost money on his land holdings but was able to get his sons into college. Thomas graduated in 1821 and Algernon in 1822, both from Transylvania University in Lexington.[57] Thomas became a popular lawyer in Nicholas County and the head of the bar.[58]

The health of both of Micah's sons began to decline, and in 1825 he decided to move his family to Huntsville, Alabama. "Thomas was sent with the blacks to Huntsville where he hired them out,"[59] followed by Micah, Dorothy and their daughter Louisiana in February 1826. Algernon was so ill that he could not travel and was left to board with a man named Hay Taliaferro in Winchester, Kentucky. By the end of the journey, Dorothy was ill and depressed. The weather had been so wet that by the time they reached Huntsville, "the town and country was almost covered with water."[60] They finally headed back north and settled in Winchester, Tennessee, "handsomely situated on the west side of the boiling fork of Elk river a few miles from the western base of the Cumberland mountains, in the County of Franklin."[61]

The day after they arrived in Winchester, Thomas returned to Kentucky to check on Algernon, who was so ill that Thomas could hardly move him to his Uncle Benjamin's house, ten miles away. Thomas wrote to his family to tell them of Algernon's condition and Dorothy and Louisiana left for Kentucky as soon as they received the letter. Algernon died not long afterward, before his father could see him again. He had just obtained a law license but had not yet begun to practice. Micah and his wife were devastated and Dorothy's health was so affected by the trip that she never recovered.[62]

Micah began to practice law in Winchester, as did his son. Thomas met his future wife, Caroline, who was the daughter of Colonel William P. Anderson of Franklin County. They were married on Thomas' birthday, March 7, 1827, when he was twenty-four years of age. Dorothy's health continued to decline and she died in December 1827 after months of terrible pain.[63] Micah wrote the following tribute to his wife in his memoirs:

I feel myself wholly incapable of doing justice to the memory of this admirable woman, the wife of my youth—in person she was small and very delicate—her weight at no time of her life exceeded 100 pounds, generally she weighed about 95; she was, however, generally very healthy—in mind she was a giantess. Her early education like my own, was limited, but she was fond of reading, and I made it a rule when at home, to read everything I did read in her hearing. As a daughter, wife, mother, mistress, friend, sister, neighbor, she was blameless. As a housekeeper she had no equal. Order and neatness everywhere prevailed. To cap the climax of her character she was a devout Christian—a member of the Baptist church. She was baptised in Cumberland river by the Rev. Thos. Chilton about the year 1810 or 1811— Her sister, *Nancy Gholson* attended her for several months in her last illness . . ."[64]

Thomas was a candidate for attorney general in the fall but lost by one vote.[65] His health was growing worse and he and his wife spent the winter in New Orleans, returning to Winchester in 1828, his health not improved. In 1827 the editor of the *Huntsville Democrat* newspaper had been killed by a prominent local attorney.[66] None of the local attorneys wanted to prosecute the case, so they approached Thomas, offering him a large fee for the job of prosecution.[67] The trial was held and the man was acquitted. The effort was too much for Thomas' health. He moved to Huntsville, where he soon ran into the man whom he had prosecuted. Only the intervention of mutual friends prevented a fight between the two. Thomas was never paid the large fee that had been promised to him.[68] Later in the year 1828, Thomas' wife Caroline gave birth to a stillborn daughter and she also died shortly after the birth.[69]

Before Caroline died, she had made arrangements for Thomas to spend the winter in Cuba for his health. He was preparing to go when he was involved in a fight in Winchester with a "furious drunken old Irishman ...which resulted in Thomas shooting him with a pistol, somewhere near the hip, which fortunately did not prove mortal."[70] Thomas at the time weighed less than 100 pounds and did not have the strength to fight the man who was threatening him, so he shot him in self defense. Micah was near enough to hear the shot and when he found out that his son had shot the Irishman, he gave Thomas a good horse and sent him away. "Several very sprightly young gentlemen began to fly about and curse and swear and call for horses, and very soon were rushing in every direction but the right one in pursuit of him."[71] Martial law was imposed upon Winchester and Micah was closely watched, but in spite of that he was able to send Thomas off to Cuba in a few days, opposing Thomas' desire to stay and stand trial.[72]

Thomas spent the winter in Cuba and his father and sister met him in Tallahassee when he returned in May of 1829. He had gained weight, his health had greatly improved, and he was determined to return to stand trial.[73] Before a trial could take place, however, Thomas was murdered on the town square in Winchester in August of 1829 by his deceased wife's brother Rufus Anderson, who did not even know Thomas well enough to recognize him.[74] Micah's wife Dorothy had been buried in the Anderson family cemetery, but her body was disinterred and buried alongside Thomas in Winchester's public cemetery. Also buried in that cemetery were the bodies of two children by his second wife.[75] Micah believed that his son's murderer was acquitted by a jury of men who went into the trial with no intention of finding him guilty, mainly due to the political influence of the defendant's father.[76] A few years later the acquitted murderer was killed in a fight with the attorney general who had prosecuted him,[77] but Micah's obsession with the injustice of the trial apparently never left him until his own death on May 27, 1850, in Mardisville, Talladega County, Alabama, about two months after he finished his memoirs.[78]

Links:
There are images of Dorothy and Micah in their FindAGrave memorials:
https://www.findagrave.com/memorial/15873610/dorothy-taul
https://www.findagrave.com/memorial/25309452/micah-taul
https://www.findagrave.com/memorial/15873630/thomas-paine-taul
https://www.findagrave.com/memorial/19699983/algernon_sidney-taul
https://www.findagrave.com/memorial/7102962/louisiana-bradford

Micah was remarried to Mary Hayter Taul. Two children.
https://www.findagrave.com/memorial/25309831/mary-taul
https://www.findagrave.com/memorial/8813238/florida-marsh
https://www.findagrave.com/memorial/25309774/victoria-taul

JOSEPH AND ISAAC CHRISMAN

Anthony₂ Gholson's daughter *Mary "Mollie"* was married to *Joseph Chrisman* who "served with George Rogers Clark in his Northwest Campaign and was with him at the capture of Vincennes."[79] George Rogers Clark was the brother of William Clark, of the Lewis and Clark expedition.

Anthony₂ Gholson's daughter *Sarah "Sally"* was married to Joseph Chrisman's brother, *Lieutenant Colonel Isaac Chrisman*.[80] Isaac Chrisman was one of the Quarter Session Judges when Micah Taul passed the examination which qualified him to become County Clerk of Wayne County, Kentucky, at age fifteen.[81]

~

BARTHOLOMEW HAYDEN

Anthony₂ Gholson's daughter *Catherine "Kitty"* was married to *Bartholomew Hayden*, who "served as a Second Lieutenant under his brother-in-law, Micah Taul, during the War of 1812."[82]

Seven: Kentuckians in the War of 1812

Samuel Gholson, son of Anthony₂
and Micah Taul, Isaac Chrisman, and Bartholomew Hayden (Haden)
Anthony₂'s Sons-in-Law

About thirty years after the end of the Revolutionary War, America again went to war against Britain. The reasons for the War of 1812 were obscure, and the war did not have the patriotic fervor behind it that the Revolutionary War had inspired. Maritime issues were a primary cause, but there was also the issue of the conquest of Canada. The idea appealed to many Americans, if for no other reason than to put a stop to the British influence over the Indians in the area.[1] Two-thirds of the occupants of the lower part of Canada were French, and the inhabitants of upper Canada were about a third American, leaving very few loyal British to carry on a war in Canada. Thomas Jefferson and other Republicans believed that Canada could be easily taken and Kentucky statesman Henry Clay bragged that the Kentucky militia alone would be able to conquer Montreal and Upper Canada.[2] Clay, who was a personal friend of *Micah Taul*[3], *Anthony₂ Gholson's* son-in-law, was young, articulate, and was elected Speaker of the House on his first day in Congress. "Staunchly nationalist and rabidly anti-British, the young Republicans regarded the Napoleonic Wars in Europe as an unparalleled opportunity to defend national honor, assert American interests, and conquer Canada and Spanish territory in Florida and the Southwest."[4] Under Clay's leadership, the War Hawks controlled the Twelfth Congress.[5] A series of events led to a war bill which was narrowly passed by Congress and signed into law by President Madison on June 18, 1812. None of the Federalists supported the bill.[6]

Two months later, Kentucky was asked to furnish volunteers. *Lieutenant Colonel Isaac Chrisman,* who was married to *Anthony₂ Gholson's* daughter *Sarah,*[7] was in charge of the regiment from Wayne County and *Micah Taul* was a major. Micah had volunteered as a private, but the men elected him to command them, and he reluctantly agreed.[8] In August of 1812, the Kentucky volunteers reported for duty, with Micah's company being attached to the regiment of Colonel Barbie, at whose residence the regiment gathered. The regiment had been ordered to go to Indiana but the orders were "changed for the northwest, in consequence of the surrender of Detroit, and the army at that place under Gen. Hull."[9] General Hull had been appointed to lead the western campaign, being the only candidate who was remotely qualified at the time. He had served with distinction in the Revolutionary War, but at age fifty-nine his body had been weakened by a stroke and his spirit by personal tragedies.[10] British General Brock managed to trick Hull into believing that all of the soldiers and civilian inhabitants of Fort Detroit would be massacred by a large group of Indians. Hull became so fearful and despondent that he surrendered the fort on August 16, 1812, without consulting any of his officers, to the disgust of everyone inside, "even the women."[11]

Winter of 1812
Micah Taul wrote in his *Memoirs*,

>The sensation in the country everywhere, at the news of "Hull's surrender" was great. I was in Lexington and saw Mr. Clay, at his house, while there he received a letter from Gen. Meigs of Ohio, containing certain intelligence of facts Allen's and Lewis's Regiment had been ordered out sometime before to re-enforce Gen. Hull, but they had not reached his headquarters before he surrendered. They were somewhere in the State of Ohio . . . We were encamped near New-port, opposite Cincinnati, a few days—our encampment was on the ground, where the town of Covington now stands, it was then a farm owned and occupied by a man of the name of Kennedy. From this place we marched to Piqua on the Miami, where we remained a week or ten days, and then moved to St. Mary's 30 miles, where we were stationed all winter.[12]

Unfortunately, the soldiers had not come prepared to stay all winter and had left home in "linen or cotton hunting shirts and pantaloons, and they were nearly worn out."[13] When winter came, the ground was covered with two feet of snow and the streams were frozen.[14]

After Hull's surrender, the popular and respected William Henry Harrison was made a major general in the militia by Kentucky leaders, even though he was not a citizen of Kentucky.[15] This obstacle, and the fact that only one major general was authorized and the position was already filled, were overcome by making him a brevet major general.[16] The Kentuckians and other westerners pressured the administration until General Harrison was given command of the army in the Northwest.[17] General Harrison appealed to Governor Shelby of Kentucky for clothing for the freezing volunteers, and around Christmas, the soldiers received an abundant supply of clothes and blankets from wives, mothers, and sisters in Kentucky. They were later able to buy supplies from the local citizens, hunt game, and build log cabin barracks.[18]

General Harrison was on the post at St. Mary's when he received a warning that he was about to be attacked by an army of British and Indians near Fort Defiance.[19]   The Kentucky troops, including Taul's regiment, marched twenty-six miles in the rain and mud to Fort Jennings on the Au Glaise the next day. The following day, General Harrison ordered Taul's regiment to return to St. Mary's, and the "forced march was the cause of much sickness and several deaths."[20]

The soldiers were able to return home after that expedition. *Taul wrote*,

> Our term of service, six months, expired, I think the first of March [1813] and we were marched to Cincinnati distant about 100 miles, paid off in part and discharged. Our friends in Wayne County met us at Cincinnati with horses. I arrived at home the third Sunday in March. The day was unusually fine for the season. We had stayed the night before at Somerset in Pulaski County from whence it was 9 miles to the Cumberland river, then the line between Wayne and Pulaski County. A large number of persons had collected on the Wayne side of the river to receive and welcome us home, and amongst them was my venerable father-in-law *Anthony[2] Gholson*, then near 80 years of age, who had rode from his residence that morning 10 or 12 miles to greet me on my return. The reception was a most cordial one. The people of the country generally were apprized of our being on the road home, and they had assembled in large numbers at the different homes on the road to see us.[21]

Micah remembered it as one of the happiest days of his life. He had returned to a healthy family and he had brought home all of the Wayne County men in his command in good health. The following day was court day and he was able to personally greet the families of the men under his command.[22]

Battle of Lake Erie, September 10, 1813

Only two months later, in June 1813, General William Henry Harrison called for 5000 mounted volunteers which again brought the Kentuckians into action.[23] The United States forces were stronger in the campaign of 1813, having more experienced officers and troops available than in 1812. General Harrison had replaced General Hull in the Northwest and Andrew Jackson was coming forth as the leader in the Southwest. Troops were paid more and legislation had been passed to make the army operate more efficiently.[24] *Micah Taul* easily raised a company in Wayne County, which included

Second Lieutenant Bartholomew Haden,[25] his brother-in-law,[26] and another brother-in-law, ***Samuel Gholson***, who was a private.[27] ***Micah*** was very proud of his company, as reflected in his memoirs:

> Some time in August we were called upon to rendezvous at Cincinnati by the 30th of the month. I immediately issued an order for my company to assemble on the day appointed at Monticello, well-mounted and prepared in all respects to take up the line of march. Accordingly on the day every man attended, well clad, and as well as I can remember well-mounted. I don't think there was an indifferent horse in the company. I am very sure there was not an indifferent man. I well remember when we marched into the city of Lexington, several of my acquaintances said to me, "Yours is the best looking and the best mounted Company that ever marched into this place." They were in a truth a noble looking set of fellows—stout, able-bodied, well-dressed Mountaineers, in fine health.[28]

Upper Canada was again targeted by the American campaign of 1813. It was very important for the Americans to gain control of the Great Lakes, especially Erie and Ontario, because the lakes provided the best way to transport troops along the northern frontier. British control of the lakes had previously gone undisputed.[29] In September 1812, Captain Isaac Chauncey was placed in command of the American naval forces on Erie and Ontario and ordered to gain control of them.[30] By the end of 1812, Chauncey had decided to focus his attention on Lake Ontario and had turned Lake Erie over to the twenty-seven-year-old Commodore Oliver H. Perry.[31] The naval commanders were short of manpower and were forced to use soldiers, including one hundred Kentucky sharpshooters furnished by General Harrison. Perry and his fleet of nine vessels sailed for Put-in-Bay in the Bass Islands at the west end of Lake Erie.[32]

On September 10, 1813, Commodore Perry, with the wind at his back, sailed his ship, the *Lawrence*, into the middle of the British fleet. He had ordered the other ships to follow him, but Lieutenant Elliott held back the *Niagara*, leaving Perry to fight the British ships unassisted. At the end of a two-hour battle with two of the largest British ships, all three of the ships were damaged and eighty percent of Perry's sailors were injured. Refusing to surrender, Perry took a rowboat over to the *Niagara*, somehow escaping injury, and assumed command. He sailed back into the British fleet of six vessels and after three hours he had killed or wounded the first and second in command on all of them.[33] This battle was the most important one fought on the Great Lakes and it allowed the United States to regain the position that was lost in 1812.[34] "Perry's message to Harrison, 'We have met the enemy and they are ours,' signaled the end of the British threat to the old Northwest."[35]

Fig. 7.1 – *Battle of Lake Erie, 1813*, U. S. Capitol painting by W. Powell , Theodor Horydczak, photographer, c.a. 1890-1971. Library of Congress No. LC-H814-T01-C01-504 DLC (b&w film dup. neg.) & detail.

Taul's company, in which *Samuel Gholson* was a sergeant,[36] "arrived at Gen. Harrison's headquarters, on the margin of Lake Erie, near the mouth of Portage River on the 11th or 12th of September just as they were landing the prisoners taken on board the British fleet on the 10th."[37] Taul described the prisoners as a "motley set of fellows, a large number of them were negroes, who had run away from their masters in the U.S."[38]

Micah said in his memoirs, "The army encamped here in a very unhealthy location several days, and I was unfortunately taken sick."[39] The science of medicine was in its very early stages, cleanliness was hard to enforce in the camps, and epidemics were common. He did not specify the nature of his illness, but diseases such as "dysentery, typhoid fever, pneumonia, malaria, measles, typhus, and even smallpox were common and often fatal."[40] Doctors "bled and blistered their patients and subjected them to assorted emetics, cathartics, and diuretics designed to purge the body of disease. . . most of the drugs were worthless or even poisonous."[41]

The detachments of soldiers were taken on small boats to Put-in-Bay, and from there to one of the smaller islands nearby. According to *Micah*, five thousand men were camped on a nine or ten acre island for two or three days, and in that length of time it became "the filthiest spot I ever saw."[42] His description:

When we landed on it, it was literally covered with snails. Here I became so much worse I could not be moved when the army was about to embark for the Canada shore, distant about nine or ten miles. I gage [gave] orders to have me put into a boat, but Gov. Shelby hearing of my situation, came to see me in company with Dr. Mitchell, his surgeon general, who gave it as his opinion, that if I was removed at that time, and put into one of the boats, that I would not reach the Canada shore alive. The Gov. peremptorily forbade my being removed. A large number besides myself and friends, who were left with me, were also left on the filthy, desolate Island, mostly without provisions, among others was Major Robert P. Henry, son of Gen. C. Henry, who like myself was too sick to be removed. A few nights afterward at a late hour, an officer of the Navy, having the command of a small vessel, called for the purpose of taking us to Detroit. He came first to my Quarters, and superintended my removal to his vessel, and afterward sent for Major Henry, who had with him a few friends. I had with me some four or five. He immediately gave orders for the vessel to sail leaving at least 100 poor fellows on the island. Maj. Henry and myself remonstrated against his sailing without taking all on board, which he could have done in perfect safety. But he was about "half seas o'er," and was deaf to our entreaties. He landed us the next day at Detroit. The poor fellows left on the Island subsisted for two or three weeks on damaged meat that had been thrown from the vessels while lying at anchor of the islands. Finding starvation staring them in the face, they ultimately got off by patching up an old boat that had been left or had drifted up on the island.[43]

Battle of the Thames, October 5, 1813

By late September of 1813, General Harrison had about 5500 men, including 3000 Kentuckians with their horses, ready for battle at the western end of Lake Erie. By the time they arrived at Detroit and Malden, the British had fled. British General Henry Procter decided to take a stand at Moraviantown, fifty miles east of Detroit, with 800 regulars and 500 Indians.[44] Procter needed to placate Tecumseh to keep him from deserting, so he promised the Indians that the army would make a stand at the fork of the Thames River. After learning that the site would not be a good location to mount a defense, Procter broke his promise and continued his eastward retreat.

An angry Tecumseh, with the help of a few of his followers and a few British soldiers, attempted to ambush the Americans at the forks. Harrison had been warned of the attack and dispersed the enemy before they could resist, and Tecumseh also retreated.[45]

Colonel Richard M. Johnson was in command of about 950 Kentucky mounted volunteers, divided into two battalions. He placed one of the battalions under his elder brother, Lieutenant Colonel James Johnson, to go against the British regulars. "Having no family, unlike his brother James, Richard Johnson reserved the more hazardous task for himself: assaulting the unpredictably dangerous Indians."[46]

> Finding the British lines thin, [Richard] Johnson asked for permission to make a frontal assault with his mounted troops. Although a cavalry charge like this was extremely unorthodox, Harrison agreed to the plan. "The American backwoodsmen ride better in the woods than any other people," he said. "I was persuaded too that the enemy would be quite unprepared for the shock and that they could not resist it."
>
> Shouting "Remember the Raisin!"—the rallying cry commemorating the massacre in January, 1813—Johnson's troops galloped toward the enemy. The right wing easily burst through the British line and then dismounted and caught the British in a crossfire, forcing them to surrender. "It is really a novel thing," said an American officer, "that raw militia stuck upon horses, with muskets in their hands instead of sabres, should be able to pierce British lines with such complete effect."[47] – Hickey, *War of 1812*

The Indians were more capable of defending their position against the Kentuckians than were the British regulars, which was not a good omen for Richard Johnson's troops. Because of the swampy condition of the battleground, the Kentuckians' horses became more of a hindrance than a help and Colonel Johnson ordered them to dismount. A fresh regiment of Kentucky militia arrived to reinforce the tired troops, making it difficult for the Indians to sustain their offensive. Colonel Johnson, as well as his horse, had been badly wounded when he was suddenly confronted by a lone Indian. The Indian fired his musket, striking Johnson on the hand, then raised his tomahawk to kill Johnson, but Johnson managed to draw his pistol and shoot the Indian in the chest. Many of those who participated in the battle stated that the Indian was Tecumseh,[48] and while some honored him, "several jubilant Kentuckians cut long strips of skin from his thighs for souvenir razor strops."[49]   It is not certain whether the Indian killed by Johnson was Tecumseh, but he was killed about that time and Colonel Johnson was given the credit for killing him, breaking the Indian confederacy and giving him the vice presidency in 1836.[50]

Fig. 7.2 – *"Remember the River Raisin!" Moraviantown, Upper Canada, October 5, 1813.* Ken Riley; National Guard Heritage. Courtesy National Guard Bureau, Department of the Army.

From *Micah Taul's* Memoirs,
    The battle of the Thames was fought on the 5th of October, 1813, and the army consisting almost exclusively of Kentucky volunteers under Harrison and Shelby, including Col. Johnson's Regiment of mounted men (the horses of the other Kentucky Volunteers had been left at Portage, returned to Sandwich in upper Canada, opposite Detroit, on the 10th of October). Many were sick and unable to march on foot and were transported across the lake in vessels furnished by Commodore Perry—But before a passage could be procured for me, the vessels were so much crowded, that I could not get in, and I had to recross the

lake in an open boat—It was then freezing cold—The weather was stormy and lake very rough, making our passage not only laborious and disagreeable but absolutely dangerous--We had two boats and about 150 men with which we coasted the lake and arrived at Portage in 6 or 7 days. Here we found the most of our horses—but in bad condition. We left for home on the 20 or 21st of October. Our encampment was in a wet prairie, near the lake—when we left the ground was frozen hard enough to bear our horses. I was something better than I had been—was able to ride a horse. The first morning after taking up the line of march for home, I was taken with the mumps, from which I did not recover until after I got home.[51]

The **Battle of the Thames** was an important victory for the Americans, undermining the British authority in the Northwest. Harrison and Perry had "turned the tide in the West and had secured the whole region to the United States."[52] Several tribes signed an armistice agreement with General Harrison on October 16.[53] **Taul's** soldiers were dismissed in Marysville and he went home to recover his health.[54]

After the defeat of Napoleon in the spring of 1814, Europe was at peace for the first time in over ten years, and Britain was able to focus its attention on punishing the Americans. The size and quality of the American army had greatly improved by the spring of 1814. Many soldiers were discharged in the winter of 1813-14, but an appealing bounty attracted many new soldiers and veterans. By early 1815, American soldiers numbered around 45,000. The Americans decided to take advantage of its control of the west and focus on Upper Canada again.[55]

A number of battles occurred during the spring of 1814 and the British were eventually able to maneuver into position to attack Washington. American officials had been slow in realizing the possibility of an attack on the nation's capital but on July 1st the president created a special military district around the area.[56] The defenders fled after they were unable to repel the attack of the British troops. Through the efforts of Dolley Madison, the cabinet records and some White House treasures were saved. On August 24, 1814, the British entered the White House, ate the dinner which had been prepared, drank the wine, collected some souvenirs and set fire to the building. They also burned the Capitol building.[57] On September 14, 1814, the British attacked Fort McHenry. Francis Scott Key had boarded a British ship to secure the release of a prisoner, and the British refused to allow him to leave until after the attack. As he paced the deck all night, watching the mortar shells exploding over the fort, he was inspired to write "The Star-Spangled Banner." The song became popular immediately, but it took more than one hundred years for Congress to make it the national anthem in 1931.[58]

Battle of New Orleans, January 8, 1815

The next British campaign was against the Gulf Coast. New Orleans was targeted with the intention of cutting off the back country of America from a seaport.[59] Andrew Jackson had assumed command of the Gulf Coast region in May of 1814. In November, he attacked the Spanish-owned seaport of Pensacola with 4100 troops and destroyed the forts, then marched to Mobile, then to New Orleans, arriving there on December 1.[60]

New Orleans in 1814 was a small but growing French-Spanish town that had only come under American domination eleven years earlier, with French and Spanish being the primary languages spoken. Houses were built close together, with the larger ones being on raised foundations to permit air circulation and prevent the wood from decaying. The streets were muddy and uncobbled, with open gutters.[61] The three most impressive buildings were the St. Louis Cathedral, the Presbytere, and the Cabildo, the latter containing the Sala Capitular, a long narrow room in which the documents were signed on December 20, 1803, transferring the Louisiana Territory from France to the United States. The Cabildo now houses the Louisiana State Museum.[62] The largest and finest house in town was built by a man named Moore and later became the Orleans Hotel.[63]

When General Jackson arrived in New Orleans on December 1, 1814, the mood of the people "radiated disloyalty and defeatism"[64] but Jackson's energy and determination soon changed their attitudes and militia began to pour in. Jackson even accepted an offer of help from the Baratarian pirates in the area, and he got along so well with Jean Laffite that Jackson made the pirate his aide-de-camp. Not only did they boost the numbers of the Americans, but they proved themselves to be skilled in artillery and familiar with the local terrain. The pirates' aid was so valuable that President Madison pardoned them after the war.[65]

When Jackson heard of the approach of the British, he took some troops to meet them well outside New Orleans. The close fighting resulted in a number of wounds. Pakenham arrived the next day with more British troops but failed to take advantage of the fact that his army was much larger than Jackson's.[66]

> This enabled Jackson to pull back unmolested and establish a
> new line behind a canal about two miles from the British. In the

days that followed, the Americans constructed earthworks along the edge of the canal between a cypress swamp on the east and the Mississippi River on the west.[67] - Hickey, *War of 1812*

Fig. 7.3 – Replica cannons on the line of defense at Chalmette National Monument, site of the Battle of New Orleans. Photo by Donna Gholson Cook, February 2002.

Fig. 7.4 – Lewis Cook with replica of cannon used in the Battle of New Orleans. Photo by Donna Gholson Cook, February 2002.

Pakenham decided to continue to New Orleans, advancing toward the well-defended American line. The British placed batteries of guns behind casks of sugar, believing that they would offer as much protection as sand, but Jackson's cannon fire penetrated the casks and killed the gunners.[68]

The British attack was begun by Colonel Thornton's routing of 700 Louisiana and Kentucky militia, followed by the main British force advancing in the fog. The fog suddenly lifted, leaving the British troops exposed, in what was described by Sir Winston Churchill as "one of the most unintelligent manœuvres in the history of British warfare."[69]

When the British got within 500 yards, the Americans began firing their cannons. When they were within 300 yards, American riflemen opened up; and when they got within 100 yards, those with muskets opened fire. "The atmosphere," said one American, "was filled with sheets of fire, and volumes of smoke." The effect of this fire—particularly the grape and canister from the American artillery—was utterly devastating. According to a British veteran of the Napoleonic Wars, it was "the most murderous [fire] I ever beheld before or since."

All along the battle line the British were mowed down before they could get near the American earthworks. Only a small column advancing along the river got to the American line, but these troops suffered such a withering fire that they had to fall back. The fire was so intense that many hardened British veterans turned and fled. Others hit the ground and remained there until the battle was over. Pakenham did his best to rally his men, but as he rode across the battlefield he made a conspicuous target. One horse was shot out from under him, and shortly after commandeering another, he was "cut asunder by a cannon ball."

General John Lambert, who took command after Pakenham fell, broke off the engagement. It had lasted only a half hour on the eastern side of the river, and yet the toll was terrific. One eyewitness said the field was a terrible sight to behold, "with dead and wounded laying in heaps"—all dressed in scarlet British uniforms. Those who had thrown themselves to the ground in the heat of battle got up when the fighting ended. A few fled but most surrendered. One officer who was far from American lines reportedly surrendered because *"these d—d Yankee riflemen can pick a squirrel's eye out as far as they can see it."*[70] – Hickey, *War of 1812*

One of these riflemen was **Samuel Gholson** of Kentucky, who was serving a six-month enlistment that began November 10, 1814, in Captain

Adam Vickery's Company of the Kentucky Detached Militia, commanded by Lieutenant Colonel Gabriel Slaughter.[71]

> Smith's *History of the Battle of New Orleans* says:
> "No troops engaged on the American side did more fatal execution upon the enemy's rank and file than did these Kentucky troops. Every man of the regiment was in rifle range and all did deadly work."[72]

Another source tells a different story about the value of the Kentucky militia to the battle. According to C. Edward Skeen in *Citizen Soldiers in the War of 1812*, the Kentuckians showed up late, ill clothed and poorly armed. Jackson was reportedly furious with their lack of order and their insubordination, and their failure to defend the right flank near the woods.[73] However...

> A court of inquiry mostly exonerated the Kentucky militia on the right bank because of a lack of arms and poor troop placement. Gen. John Adair, who commanded the Kentuckians on the right bank, sought to get Jackson to withdraw his harsh judgment of the Kentuckians. Jackson, however, refused to concede Adair's point, and this triggered an angry response in the press in Kentucky that lasted many years and was dredged up again during Jackson's presidential campaigns in 1824, 1828, and 1832.[74]

Ironically, the **Battle of New Orleans** was fought on January 8, 1815, two weeks after the Treaty of Ghent had been signed on December 24, 1814,[75] to end the war. "The British lost over 2,000 men (including close to 500 captured). The United States, by contrast, lost only about 70 men, and only 13 on Jackson's side of the river."[76] The battle preserved America's claim to the Louisiana Purchase, but the war accomplished very little. It did, however, enhance the reputations of a number of participants, "helping catapult four men into the presidency—James Monroe, John Quincy Adams, Andrew Jackson, and William Henry Harrison—and three men into the vice-presidency--Daniel D. Tompkins, John C. Calhoun, and Richard M. Johnson."[77] It boosted the career of others including Henry Clay, and it sent **Micah Taul** to Congress in 1814.[78] Despite few concrete achievements, the War of 1812 was significant because "it promoted national self-confidence and encouraged the heady expansionism that lay at the heart of American foreign policy for the rest of the century."[79]

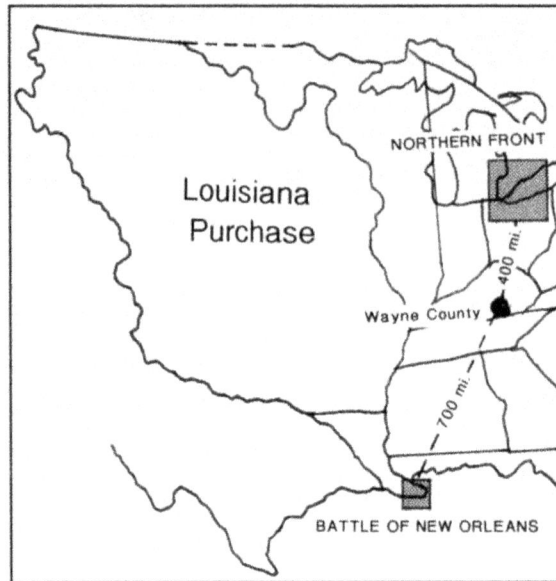

Map 3
Kentucky Militia Involvement in the War of 1812.
The United States in 1810. Map drawn by D. Cook.
Copyright 2003.

Map 4
War of 1812, Northern Front activities involving
the militia of Wayne County, Kentucky.
Map drawn by D. Cook. Copyright 2003.

Eight: Chasing Gholson Ghosts

After I published my first book, I had an opportunity to take a road trip through the areas in Virginia and Kentucky where my Gholson ancestors lived. I especially wanted to try to find the location of the original land grant in Virginia from King George II and the cemetery in Kentucky where *Anthony₂* and his wife *Elizabeth* were buried. The drive through Cumberland Gap is beautiful today, but I can't imagine how difficult it must have been in 1801 when the Gholson family moved from Virginia to Kentucky. The trip fulfilled my dreams beyond my wildest hopes. I would like to share my photos and descriptions with my Gholson cousins, near and far.

~

Chasing Gholson Ghosts
Through Virginia and Kentucky
by Donna Gholson Cook
Research Trip, October 17-22, 2005

If you're reading this, there is a good chance that you have been bitten by the genealogy bug. I have been fascinated since childhood by stories of my father's family and their cowboy days in early Texas. I also knew that my Gholson ancestors were among the earliest American colonists but did not realize until recently that they were closely connected with some of the major events in American history. In my research, I discovered early Virginia land grants from King George II, a mention of *Anthony Gholson* in a letter written by George Washington, and connections between *Anthony* and Patrick Henry's relatives.

About 25 years ago, I began to seriously research my ancestors and compile the information into my first book, *Gholson Road: Revolutionaries and Texas Rangers*, published in 2004. While researching the book, I visited and photographed sites in Texas and Louisiana. One additional thing that I had always wanted to do was to take a trip through Virginia and Kentucky to trace the migration path of my Gholson ancestors and the ancestors of thousands of other Texans.

In connection with an astronomy trip to Boston with my hubby Lew, I cooked up a plan to visit some Gholson ancestral sites and asked him to accompany me on a six-day road trip beginning at Jamestown, site of the first European colony in Virginia. Dr. Theodore Gulston, a London physician related to the first Gholsons who came to America, was one of the investors in the Virginia Company of London, which financed the first Virginia colonies. In 1616, visitors to Dr. Gulston's London home from Virginia included Sir Thomas Dale and Uttomakin, counsellor to Powhatan, the father of Pocahontas.

Our next stop was St. John's Church in Richmond, Virginia. I have long been fascinated with Patrick Henry and his speech that lit the fire of the American Revolution, and it was a thrill to visit the actual church where the 2nd Virginia Convention was held. The church building has been expanded several times from the tiny original building, which is the central portion of the photo on the right, below. The delegates entered through the door shown in the photo.

From Richmond, we drove north to the Piedmont section of Virginia, north of the present Lake Anna on the Orange-Spotsylvania county line. In 1728, *Anthony₁ Gholson* was given a grant of 1000 acres by King George II (along the present Virginia State Highway 601, photo below, left), and his sons *William* and *Anthony, Jr.* were jointly given an adjacent 1000 acres. *William's* son, *Anthony₂*, rented land from George Washington in Frederick County from 1768-1786. Washington, in a letter to his brother, referred to *Anthony₂'s* failure to pay his rent for several years, prompting my husband to tell me that I qualify for the DAR—Deadbeats of the American Revolution!

Patrick Henry is sometimes referred to as *The Voice* and George Washington as *The Sword* of the Revolution. Thomas Jefferson, another contemporary of Anthony Gholson, is sometimes called *The Pen*. A trip through Virginia would not be complete without a stop at Charlottesville to visit Monticello, Jefferson's home (above, right). The house is a construction marvel and the location is absolutely beautiful. Thomas Jefferson was a true genius who spent every moment of his life trying to improve the world around him, keeping meticulous records of everything he did and everything he observed, including plant studies from his large garden.

We drove north on Skyline Drive from I-64 to U.S. Highway 33. To the west, in the Shenandoah Valley, is Augusta County as seen from Skyline Drive (below). *Anthony₂ Gholson* (grandson of *Anthony₁*) lived there during the time of the Revolutionary War and was a member of Captain Tate's Augusta County militia.

Anthony₂ moved to Botetourt County around 1779 and lived in the area north of Roanoke before moving to Wayne County, Kentucky in 1801. In 1797, he was granted permission to build a grist mill on his land on the branch coming into Tinker Creek from the foot of Fullheart's Knob (below, left). He bought 680 acres of land from Reverend Caleb Wallace and his wife, Rosanna, whose brother was married to the sister of Patrick Henry.

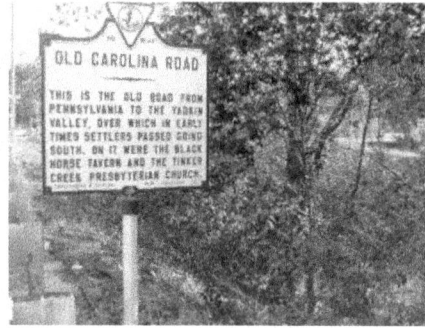

An 18 x 24 log house was built for the reception of deer skins and hemp, and *Anthony₂* was appointed inspector for the skins and hemp received, which were accepted as payment of taxes in the county. The location of this house was at or near the forks of the Carolina Road (above, right) and the original Carvin road.

In driving along the old Carolina Road (now Highway 11 or Lee Highway) we stopped to take photos of a small creek (above) and a van turned into a driveway near our parked car. We introduced ourselves to the driver, who owned the property, and told him that we were interested in the history of the area. He graciously showed us around and took us to the creek where he had found what he believed to be the foundation of an old grist mill. It is entirely possible that the mill was *Anthony₂'s*, as the location fits the description in the original records. *Anthony₂* lived in the immediate area with his family for 22 years, then in 1801 followed Daniel Boone's route, along with thousands of others who passed through Cumberland Gap.

Cumberland Gap

Facing West:

Facing East:

One of the places I most wanted to see on this trip was the location of *Anthony₂'s* home in Steubenville, Kentucky, and the Baptist church and cemetery for which he donated land. Steubenville Baptist Church has moved and the building is now the home of Pleasant Valley Baptist Church (below, left). *Anthony₂* and his wife **Elizabeth** are buried in the cemetery beside the church (below, left and right), but the exact locations of their graves are unknown. A memorial was added to honor *Anthony₂* not long after our visit. *Anthony₂'s* house was built in 1801 and stood until 1977, when it burned to the ground. A local resident told us that the chimney rocks from the house were used to build a retaining wall in front of a nearby house (below).

Armed with a map from the courthouse, we were able to find the location where *Anthony₂'s* house stood. As I was walking around on the vacant lot, the neighbors came out of their house. I did not know whether I was going to be scolded or shot for trespassing, and it was a relief to learn that they were very nice, friendly people. Below is a view of the location of *Anthony₂'s* house when we were there. Below that photo is a photo of the house before it burned (photo courtesy of the Wayne County Historical Society).

A special thanks to my husband Lew for accompanying me on the chase of my ancestors' ghosts and supporting and encouraging me every step of the way in my obsession with family history!

Donna Gholson Cook
www.gholson-cook.com

Note: **Anthony₂'s** son **Samuel** *(my 3ʳᵈ-great-grandfather) moved to what later became Texas in 1832 with his son* **Albert.** **Samuel,** *his son, and his grandsons* **B. F. (Frank) Gholson** *and* **Sam S. Gholson** *were among the first Texas Rangers and early ranchers in Central Texas.* **Anthony₂'s** *descendants probably number in the thousands by now, all with interesting stories of their own. I hope this will encourage some of them to tell their own stories.*

One additional note: Many years ago, in July 1968, I took a trip to visit friends in Ohio, and they suggested that we take a boat trip from Put-in-Bay to the island where the monument to Commodore Perry stands. It was a beautiful day and a very interesting trip, but I wish I had known at the time that I had an ancestor who was there very soon after the Battle of Lake Erie in the War of 1812!

DGC

Appendix 1

Virginia Land Grant from King George II
to Anthony[1] Gholson

Enlarged lower left corner, shown in Chapter 3 as Fig. 3.1:

Full pages 441 and 442 follow.

Fig. 3.1 is a sample corner of the land grant to Anthony Gholston for 1000 acres by King George II. State Records, Land Office (RG4) Register of the Land Office, Original Patents and Grants 1728-1933, Patent Book 13: 1725-1730 [Microfilm Reel 12] 1000 acre grant to Anthony Gholson, 28 September 1728, pp 441-2. Archives Research Services, The Library of Virginia, Richmond, VA.

George the Second &c To all &c Whereas &c We have given granted and
confirmed and by these presents for us our heirs and successors Do give grant and confirm unto
Matthew Hart of Prince George County one certain tract or parcel of land containing six hundred
and twenty three acres lying and being on the South side of Little Sollowny and on the South side
of the Rocky Creek in the County of Brunswick aforesaid and bounded as followeth (to wit)
Begining at a White oak on a Bowerpond thence South two hundred and forty six poles to a
corner hickory thence West thirty one degrees South three hundred and forty poles to a small Red
oak thence North three hundred and eighty six poles to the Creek thence Down the creek as it
Meanders to the Begining With all &c to have hold &c to be hold &c yielding and paying &c
Provided &c In witness &c Witness Our Trusty and Welbeloved William Gooch Esqr Our Lieut Govr
and Commander in Chief of our said Colony and Dominion at Williamsburgh under the Seal of our
said Colony the twenty eighth day of September one thousand seven hundred and twenty eight
in the Second year of our Reign
                                                William Gooch

George the Second &c To all &c Whereas &c We have given granted and
confirmed and by these presents for us our heirs and successors Do give grant and confirm unto
James Williams of Prince George County one certain tract or parcel of land containing Two
hundred and sixty one acres lying and being on the South side of Sollowny River in
Brunswick County and bounded as followeth (to wit) Begining at a White oak and
two small hiccorys near the Mouth of Walls Sawpen Branch thence South sixteen degrees
East one hundred and seventeen poles to a corner hiccory thence East twenty nine degrees
South two hundred and sixty six poles to a corner Butterwood in a slash thence North
twenty three degrees East fifty two poles to two small hiccorys upon the River thence up
the River north as it Meanders to the Begining With all &c to have hold &c to be hold &c
yielding and paying &c Provided &c In witness &c Witness our Trusty and Welbeloved
William Gooch Esqr Our Lieut Governor and Commander in Chief of our said Colony and
Dominion at Williamsburgh under the Seal of our said Colony the twenty eighth day of
September one thousand seven hundred and twenty eight in the Second year of our Reign
                                                William Gooch

George the Second &c To all &c Whereas &c We have given granted and
confirmed and by these presents for us our heirs and successors Do give grant and confirm unto
John Wall Jun of Brunswick County one certain tract or parcel of land Containing three
hundred and eighty seven acres lying and being on the South side of Mahorin River in the
County of Brunswick aforesaid and bounded as followeth (to wit) Begining at a White
oak on the East side of the great Creek below Curstianna Hort on the Indian line thence by
the Indian line East two hundred and eighty poles to a White oak thence South and by West
one hundred eighty four poles to a Spanish oak thence South West two hundred and twenty
poles to a Red oak thence North West thirty seven poles to a White oak thence North seventy
three poles to a Red oak thence North twenty degrees West one hundred and seventy four poles
to a Red oak thence North sixty two poles to a White oak thence North — degrees East
fourteen poles to the Begining With all &c to have hold &c to be hold &c yielding and
paying &c Provided &c In witness &c Witness our Trusty and Welbeloved William Gooch
Esqr our Lieut Governor and Commander in Chief of our said Colony and Dominion at
Williamsburgh under the Seal of our said Colony the twenty eighth day of September one
thousand seven hundred and twenty eight in the Second year of our Reign
                                                William Gooch

George the Second &c To all &c Whereas &c We have given granted and
confirmed and by these presents for us our heirs and successors Do give grant and confirm unto
Anthony Sheldon of Spotsylvania County one certain tract or parcel of land containing one —

thousand Acres lying and being on the Branches of Plentifull and Terry Runn Saint George's parish in the County of Spotsylvania aforesaid and bounded as followeth (to wit)

Beginning at two Corner White Oaks on the South East Side of Plentifull in Mr Camms line thence North fifty five West three hundred and ninety poles to a Corner White Oak of Wareh and others on the South East side of Glendros path thence North twenty one East three hundred and seventy poles to a White Oak Red Oak and Spanish Oak on a stoney Ridge thence South fifty nine East four hundred and forty four poles to a small White Oak and hickory standing near Col. Corbins line on a Ridge thence South thirty one West two hundred and sixty four poles to three Corner White Oaks of Mr Camms and Col. Corbins standing on a Ridge thence South thirty five degrees West one hundred and thirty six poles to the Beginning **Withall** we have held or to be held or yielding and paying &c Provided &c In Witness &c Witness our Trusty and Welbeloved William Gooch Esq. our Lieut Governor and Commander in Chief of our said Colony and Dominion at Williamsburgh under the Seal of our said Colony the twenty eighth day of September one thousand seven hundred and twenty eight in the Second Year of our Reign

William Gooch

George the Second &c **To All &c Know Ye** that for divers good Causes and Considerations but more Especially for and in Consideration of the Sum of fifteen shillings of good and Lawfull Money for our use paid to our Receiver General of our Revenues in this our Colony and Dominion of Virginia **We Have** given granted and Confirmed and by these presents for us our heirs and successors Do give grant and Confirm unto John Cunningham of Prince George County one Certain Tract or parcell of Land Containing one hundred and fifty acres lying and being on the North Side of the Stoney Creek in the County aforesaid and bounded as followeth (to wit) **Beginning** at a poplar above the Mouth of a small Spring Branch above his field near a pond Rocks thence North one hundred and fifty four poles to a Corner thence East one hundred and eight poles to a Corner thence South two hundred and thirty two poles to Stony Creek thence up the Creek as it Meanders to the Beginning **Withall** we have held or to be held or yielding and paying &c Provided &c In Witness &c Witness our Trusty and Welbeloved William Gooch Esq. our Lieut Governor and Commander in Chief of our said Colony and Dominion at Williamsburgh under the Seal of our said Colony the twenty eighth day of September one thousand seven hundred and twenty eight in the Second year of our Reign

William Gooch

George the Second &c **To All &c Whereas &c We Have** given granted Confirmed and by these presents for us our heirs and successors Do give grant and Confirm unto Bartholomew Wood of Saint George's parish in Spotsylvania County one Certain Tract or parcell of Land Containing two hundred and eighty six acres lying and being on a Ridge between Rappahannock and Mattapony Rivers in the parish and County aforesaid and bounded as followeth (to wit) **Beginning** at a King Oak in William Johnstons line and born a to William Tapp and Runns thence North four degrees West three hundred poles to a large Red Oak a black oak and hickory Saplin Corner to the said William Johnstons thence North fifty eight degrees East one hundred and seventy four poles to a White Oak on the Side of a Valley thence South fifty eight degrees East two hundred and sixty poles to a pine in a poyson old field thence South twenty degrees East one hundred and sixty poles to a White oak Corner to Mr francis and Anthony Thorntons old patent and John James thence South sixty one degrees West three hundred poles to a black Gum and Maple on the South Side of a Branch of Rassapanax and born a to William Tapp thence North seventy four degrees West one hundred and forty poles to the Beginning **Withall** we have hold or to be held or yielding and paying &c Provided &c In Witness &c Witness our Trusty and Welbeloved William Gooch Esq. our

Appendix 2

The Family of Anthony$_2$ Gholson
and Elizabeth Sandidge

Sources:

1. *Gholson and Allied Families, A Revised Golden Anniversary Edition*
Compiled by Ronald Lee Gholson, 2000, reprint of *Gholson and Allied Families* by Virginia Baker Mitchell, 1950, with additional information.
2. I searched the *FindAGrave.com* website for each family member, making changes as needed and adding links for those listed. That website is more reliable than most, with many photos of headstones, but the main flaw is that information is often incomplete, especially names of children. For example, only two children are listed under **Anthony$_2$**'s memorial, but he and his wife **Elizabeth** had a very large family. I have requested that the others be added to the website. I attempted to find additional information for those family members whose details are very few, but there is so much conflicting information in all of the different websites that I decided to leave it to the descendants of each family member if more information is desired.

(Parents' names in parentheses)

Generation 1:
William$_1$ Gholson was probably the first in this line to come to America in 1675.

Generation 2:
Anthony$_1$ Gholson (William$_1$ Gholson) lived in Virginia, born 1685, died 1764, married **Jane** _____, children **William, Elizabeth, Lucy, John, Anthony, Jr.**

Generation 3:
William$_2$ Gholson (Anthony$_1$ Gholson) lived in Virginia, born 1705/6, died 1800. **(William$_2$ Gholson** had a brother named **Anthony, Jr.)**

Generation 4:
Anthony$_2$ Gholson (William$_2$ Gholson) born Virginia 1733, married **Elizabeth Sandidge** Virginia c. 1760. **Anthony$_2$** died in Wayne County,

Kentucky 1815. **Elizabeth** died 1810/1817. Their bodies were interred in unmarked graves in Steubenville Cemetery, Wayne County, Kentucky. A cemetery marker was added May 6, 2006, to honor **Anthony₂**. Information concerning the ceremony was in the May 17, 2006 *Wayne County Outlook,* which can be accessed on the Wayne County Public Library's website. https://www.findagrave.com/memorial/41172835/anthony-gholson

Note in FindAGrave memorial: Private under Captain James Tate in the Augusta Co. VA, militia during the Revolutionary War.

Anthony₂ Gholson and **Elizabeth Sandidge** had the following children:

1.   **Francis Gholson**, born 1760
2.   **William³ Gholson**, born circa 1764
3.   **Mary "Mollie" Gholson**, born circa 1766
4.   **Sarah "Sally" Gholson**, born circa 1768
5.   **Elizabeth "Betty" Gholson**, born circa 1770
6.   **Samuel Gholson**, born circa 1772
7.   **John Gholson**, born 8 February 1775
8.   **James Gholson**, born 26 September 1776
9.   **J. Benjamin Gholson**, born 1777
10.   **Nancy Gholson**, born circa 1778
11.   **Catherine "Kitty" Gholson**, born circa 1780
12.   **Dorothy "Dolly" Gholson**, born 1786

_____

Details for each of those listed above:

1.   **Francis Gholson**, born circa 1760, married **Mary Craig** in Hamilton County, Illinois circa 1782. **Mary** was born in Virginia 17 July 1760. She was the daughter of Toliver Craig and Elizabeth Johnson. **Francis** moved to Kentucky, then briefly to Maurey County, Tennessee, then to Hamilton County, Illinois. **Mary** died 1820. **Francis** died 1825 in Walpole, Hamilton County, Illinois.
Francis Gholson:
https://www.findagrave.com/memorial/58024196/francis-gholson
Mary Craig Gholson:
https://www.findagrave.com/memorial/198036072/mary-gholson
Francis Gholson and **Mary Craig** had many children, but there is an unresolved discrepancy. The twins **Julie** and **James** could not have been born four months after the birth of **John** to the same mother.

i. **John Gholson**, born 8 February 1784, Virginia, died 1827, Hamilton County, Illinois.
   https://www.findagrave.com/memorial/198036160/john-gholson
ii. **Julie Gholson** was born May 1784.
iii. **James Gholson** was born May 1784.
iv. **Elizabeth "Betsy" Gholson,** born Virginia 1785.
v. **Nathaniel Gholson,** born 25 February 1787, Fayette County, Kentucky, died 12 February 1851 Henry County, Iowa.
   https://www.findagrave.com/memorial/32371561/nathaniel-s_-gholson
vi. **William₄ Gholson** was born 20 April 1789, Fayette County, Kentucky, married **Sarah Thomas** 1810, died 4 August 1843, Hamilton County, Illinois. Eight children: Sallie, Harvey, Milton, William Thomas, Marine Francis, Eli, James T., and W. Asbury.
   https://www.findagrave.com/memorial/59543052/william-gholson
   https://www.findagrave.com/memorial/55078268/sarah-gholson
vii. **Sarah "Sallie" Gholson,** born Kentucky 01 January 1791.
viii. **Lydia Gholson**, born Kentucky 15 June 1792, died 1 July 1850, Hamilton County, Illinois.
   https://www.findagrave.com/memorial/55469693/lydia-rice
ix. **Benjamin Gholson** was born 17 December 1793.
x. **Toliver Craig Gholson,** born Kentucky 11 June 1797.
xi. **Paris Lee Gholson,** born 22 September 1798.

———————

2. **William³ Gholson**, born Virginia circa 1764, married **Mary Cross** in Botetourt County, Virginia 9 December 1784. **William³** and **Mary** had the following child:
   i. **Catherine Gholson**, born circa 1785, married **Anthony B. Hackett** 1803.

———————

3. **Mary "Mollie" Gholson**, born Virginia circa 1766, married **Joseph Chrisman** in Botetourt County, Virginia 23 August 1788.

———————

4. **Sarah "Sally" Gholson**, born Virginia circa 1768, married **Isaac Chrisman** in Botetourt County, Virginia 22 May 1788. **Isaac Chrisman** married 2nd Elizabeth Stephens. FindAGrave contains an entry for Elizabeth, and none for Sarah, but names **Sarah** as the first wife of **Isaac**.
https://www.findagrave.com/memorial/91068045/isaac-chrisman

Sarah and **Isaac Chrisman** had eight children:
  i.   **Elizabeth Chrisman**, married **John Dick**, 03 March 1806,
       Elizabeth died 27 August 1876.
       https://www.findagrave.com/memorial/68400589/elizabeth-dick
  ii. **Harvey Chrisman**
  iii. **Cornelius "Neely" Chrisman**
  iv. **Dorothy Chrisman**
  v.   **Charley Chrisman**
  vi. **Susannah "Suky" Chrisman**
       https://www.findagrave.com/memorial/40911067/susannah-barrier
  vii. **John Chrisman**
  viii. **Jane Chrisman,** married **Samuel Cecil** in Wayne County,
        Kentucky, 16 August 1806.

———

5.   **Elizabeth "Betty" Gholson**, born Virginia circa 1770, married twice,
first to **James Neely**, second to **William Neely** in Botetourt County,
Virginia 01 December 1789. **Elizabeth** and **William** had one child:
  i.   **Westley Woodford Neely**, born 1793
       https://www.findagrave.com/memorial/26870692/wesley-woodford-neely

———

6.   **Samuel Gholson**, born Virginia circa 1772 married **Mary Ann
     "Polly" Slaton** 24 June 1801. **Samuel** and **Mary Ann** had five
     children.
  i.   **Angeline Gholson** married **Jenkin Williams** in Arkansas and
       lived there until she died.
  ii. **Alvades Gholson** died in his twenties in 1829 at Exelet, Illinois
       when he was thrown from a horse and killed.
  iii. **Alhanon Gholson** was robbed and killed in Santa Fe in the fall
       of 1827.
  iv. **Alvira Gholson** died unmarried at age seventeen.
  v.   **Albert Gholson**, born in Kentucky 25 May 1818. He was
       fourteen when he moved to Texas with his father, **Samuel**, two
       of the first Texas settlers. **Albert** died 10 June 1860, after
       being shot by a neighbor and was buried on his ranch.
       He had two children with his first wife, **Elydia Anderson**, who
       died when their children were very young, and three with his
       second wife, **Mary A. Mathis**. Albert died when their children
       were young. More information about Albert and his

descendants is found in *Gholson Brothers In the Thick of It,* by Donna Gholson Cook.

––––––––––

7.   **John Gholson**, born Virginia 8 February 1775, married **Lucretia Griffith** in Botetourt County, Virginia 3 March 1794. Moved to Wayne County, Kentucky, with his parents 1801, then Maury County, Tennessee, and back to Wayne County by age 75. Died c. 1850. Buried Wayne County, Hutchison Graveyard No. 1, unmarked grave. Served in the War of 1812 under Captains Micah Taul and Thomas Miller. **John** and **Lucretia** had the following children:

    i.   **Anna Gholson**.
    ii.   **Anthony Gholson**, resided in Bell County, Texas.
    iii.   **Margaret Gholson**, married **George William Moore**.
    iv.   **Hannah Gholson**, married **Anthony Harper** 4 May 1823.
    v.   **Nancy Gholson**, born 3 January 1802.
    vi.   **Susan Gholson** born 23 April 1804, died 2 July 1872, m. **Andrew McBeath**.
        https://www.findagrave.com/memorial/65325980/susan-mcbeath
        https://www.findagrave.com/memorial/65325903/andrew-mcbeath
    vii.   **Eliza M. Gholson**, married **William B. Ament** 1 Nov 1824.
    viii.   **Malinda Gholson**, married **Thomas Ament** 9 October 1824.
    ix.   **Everett Gholson**.

––––––––––

8.   **James Gholson**, born Virginia 26 September **1776,** married **Martha "Patsy" Lewis** in Lincoln County, Kentucky 4 Feb 1796. **Martha "Patsy"** was born Oct 1775, and died Aug 1836. **James** died 22 September 1853 in Jackson, Madison County, Tennessee, at 76 years of age. **James** was a captain and a major in the War of 1812. Micah Taul speaks of him as his wife's brother "of Cumberland County, Kentucky" shortly after the War of 1812. **James Gholson** and **Martha "Patsy" Lewis** had the following child:

    i.   **Milton G. Gholson,** born 11 March 1814.

––––––––––

9.   **J. Benjamin Gholson**, born Virginia 1777, married **Mary "Polly" Hayden** in Wayne County, Kentucky, 18 Nov 1803. **Mary** was born 1779, died 1851 in Cherokee County, Texas. **Benjamin** died 1854 in Cherokee County, Texas. His body was interred in Mixon, Texas. At approximately 24 years old, **Benjamin** came to Wayne County, Kentucky with his parents.

In 1811 he was appointed Coroner to fill the vacancy by resignation of his brother-in-law Bartholomew Hayden.

*Author's note: In previous lists, **Benjamin's** birth date was given as "circa 1782" which would have made him younger than sisters **Nancy** and **Catherine**. Since his headstone gives his birth year as 1777, he has been moved up to #9, older than **Nancy** and **Catherine**.*

J. Benjamin Gholson
https://www.findagrave.com/memorial/24791908/j_-benjamin-gholson
Mary D. Hayden
https://www.findagrave.com/memorial/24791941/mary-d_-gholson

J. Benjamin Gholson and **Mary "Polly" Hayden** had the following children:

- i. **Harriet H. Gholson,** married **Harvey Hoge** in Somerset, Pulaski County, Kentucky, 31 October 1827.
- ii. **Arustus Hayden Gholson Sr.,** born 9 February 1805, d. 1872.
  https://www.findagrave.com/memorial/71542654/arustus-hayden-gholson
- iii. **Cynthian Gholson, m**arried James Campbell in Logan County, Kentucky 05 January 1837.

---

10. **Nancy Gholson**, born Virginia circa 1778.

---

11. **Catherine "Kitty" Gholson**, born Virginia circa 1780, married **Bartholomew Hayden** in Botetourt County, Virginia, 14 June 1801. **Bartholomew** was born in Virginia 21 August 1776. **Bartholomew** died 11 December 1845 at 69 years of age. According to Augusta Phillips Johnson's *A Century of Wayne County, Kentucky, 1800-1900,* Anthony₂ Gholson reared two of his grandchildren after the death of their mother, **Catherine**. **Catherine "Kitty" Gholson** and **Bartholomew Hayden** had the following children:

- i. **Anthony Hayden**
- ii. **Julia Gholson Hayden Buster** b. 1802, d. 16 April 1829 (age 27) m. Joshua Buster.
  https://www.findagrave.com/memorial/40695693
- iii. **Augustus Hayden** born 31 July 1804, died 20 March 1833 in Wayne County, Kentucky, at 28 years of age. His body was interred in Wayne County, Kentucky, Molen, Old Dibrell Buck Cemetery. He married **Martha Burton Dibrell** in Wayne County Kentucky 13 October 1825.

https://www.findagrave.com/memorial/126195019/augustus-haden lists him as son of **Julia Gholson** and **Bartholomew Hayden**, but this is probably an error. He has a sister named Julia.

---

12. **Dorothy "Dolly" Gholson**, born 1786, married **Micah Taul** May 22, 1802, **Dorothy** died December 1827 in Franklin County, Tennessee. **Micah Taul** died 27 May 1850. Their likenesses can be found in FindAGrave:
https://www.findagrave.com/memorial/15873610/dorothy-taul
https://www.findagrave.com/memorial/25309452/micah-taul
Children of **Dorothy "Dolly" Gholson** and **Micah Taul**:

i.   **Thomas Paine Taul**, born 1802, died 26 August 1829, Winchester, Franklin County, Tennessee.
https://www.findagrave.com/memorial/15873630/thomas-paine-taul

ii.   **Algernon Sidney Taul** born 21 Oct 1804, died 1 May 1826 Clark County, Kentucky.
https://www.findagrave.com/memorial/19699983/algernon_sidney-taul

iii.   **Louisiana Taul Bradford** born 1808, died 1863, Talladega County, Alabama, married **Jacob Tipton Bradford**
https://www.findagrave.com/memorial/7102962/louisiana-bradford
Children of **Louisiana Taul Bradford** and **Jacob Tipton Bradford:**

a.   **Darthula Maria Bradford Wilson**, born 19 October 1832, died 9 May 1859, Talladega County, Alabama
https://www.findagrave.com/memorial/7102732/darthula-maria-wilson

b.   **Taul Bradford**, born 20 January 1835, died 28 October 1883, Talladega County, Alabama
https://www.findagrave.com/memorial/7365976/taul-bradford

c.   **Francina Bobbins Hardie Bradford** born 4 February County, Alabama, married **James White Hardie** 1856, Francina died 13 June 1863 (age 26)
https://www.findagrave.com/memorial/7102861/francina-bobbins-bradford

d.   **Tipton Bradford** born 22 April 1839, died 21 January 1892, Tuscaloosa County, Alabama, m. **Jennie _____** Bradford
https://www.findagrave.com/memorial/194487001/tipton-bradford

e.   **Mary Hardie Bradford** born 4 April 1841, died 2 December 1854 (age 13) Talladega County, Alabama
https://www.findagrave.com/memorial/153709434/mary-hardie-bradford

Note in Micah Taul Memorial:
https://www.findagrave.com/memorial/25309452/micah-taul
US Congressman. His parents moved to Wayne County, Kentucky in 1787, where he attended a private school, studied law, and began a practice in 1801, when he was only 16 years old. In 1801 he was also appointed Clerk of the Wayne County Court. During the War of 1812 Taul served as commander of the Wayne County Volunteers with the rank of Colonel, and his unit saw action as part of General William Harrison's force that fought the British along Lake Erie. In 1814 he was elected to the US House of Representatives as a Democratic-Republican and served one term, 1815 to 1817. He did not run for reelection in 1816 and resumed practicing law. In 1826 he moved to Winchester, Tennessee, where he continued to practice law. In 1846 Taul relocated to Mardisville, Alabama, where he practiced law and owned a plantation. Micah Taul was the father of Micah Taul (1832-1873), who served as Alabama Secretary of State and a member of the state Railroad Commission, and the grandfather of Taul Bradford (1835-1883), who also served in Congress.
Bio by: Bill McKern

Note in Thomas Paine Taul Memorial:
https://www.findagrave.com/memorial/15873630/thomas-paine-taul
Son of Dorothy and Micah Taul. Aged 27 years.
One of the most dramatic and lasting of all the historic episodes in the history of Franklin County was the killing of Tom Taul and the trial of Rufus K. Anderson as the murderer. The incident created social and political estrangements that lingered for many years afterward. Rufus K. Anderson was the son of Col. Wm. P. Anderson and the Andersons were wealthy and aristocratic. Thomas P. Taul was the son of Col. Micah Taul, who had been a colonel in the war of 1812 and a member of Congress from Kentucky. Coming to Tennessee, he located at Winchester, and soon took rank among the first lawyers of the State, and he and Hopkins L. Turney were then the leading members of the Winchester bar. Tom Taul is said to have been the most brilliant young lawyer in Tennessee at that time. He married Miss Caroline, the accomplished daughter of Col. Wm. P. Anderson, and sister of Rufus K. In a few years Mrs. Taul died of consumption, childless and gave her property to her husband by a deed. After her death the Andersons claimed that Taul had never been kind to her and that he had coerced the deed. Rufus K. Anderson, a young man of the highest notions of civil life, had gone to Alabama before his sister's marriage and before Col. Taul moved to Tennessee, and had never seen his brother-in-law, Tom Taul. After

the death of his sister, he returned to Winchester, and asked to have Tom Taul pointed out to him, which being done, he walked across the street to where Taul was standing, and shot and killed him. The trial came off in less than a year and Col. Taul employed Col. Sam Laughlin, a most powerful prosecuting lawyer, and other lawyers of distinction to prosecute Anderson, who was defended by Hon. Felix Grundy, Hopkins L. Turney and other distinguished lawyers. By the time the trial came on the whole county was divided under the respective banners of the contending parties. The jury returned a verdict of "not guilty." Whether the verdict was just, or whether the jury was led to commit an error, will never be known with certainty. (from Goodspeed's History).

Note in Taul Bradford Memorial:
https://www.findagrave.com/memorial/7365976/taul-bradford
U.S. Congressman. After graduating from the University of Alabama, in 1854, he studied law, was admitted to the bar in 1855 and commenced to practice law in Talladega, Alabama. During the Civil War, he served in the Confederate Army as a Major in the 10th Regiment, Alabama Infantry and later as a Lieutenant Colonel in command of the 13th Regiment, Alabama Infantry. After the war, he was a member of the Alabama State House of Representatives, (1871-72) and was elected as a Democrat to the Forty-fourth Congress, serving (1875-77). Not a candidate for re-nomination, he continued the practice of law until his death at age 48.
Bio by: John "J-Cat" Griffith

Appendix 3

Number of Gholson Graves by State in U.S.
Including Maiden Names
As of April 8, 2020

In searching for Gholson graves in the FindAGrave.com website, I found **Gholsons** in 39 states and the District of Columbia. The following list is a fair indication of the dispersal of descendants of **Anthony**[1] and many of those are also descendants of **Anthony**[2]. The grave of **Anthony**[2] **Gholson**, who died in 1815, is one of the oldest **Gholson** graves in the website.
https://www.findagrave.com/memorial/41172835/anthony-gholson

Number of Gholsons in U.S. cemeteries:
https://www.findagrave.com/memorial/search?firstname=&middlename=&lastname=Gholson&birthyear=&birthyearfilter=&deathyear=&deathyearfilter=&location=&locationId=country_4&memorialid=&datefilter=&orderby=c&includeMaidenName=true&page=109#sr-100384628

Number of Gholson graves by state in descending order:

Texas	398
Illinois	295
Kentucky	277
Virginia	187
Missouri	127
California	85
Iowa	68
Tennessee	68
Mississippi	67
Ohio	67
Georgia	58
Arkansas	49
Washington	48
Alabama	45
Indiana	44
North Carolina	44
Kansas	32
Oregon	31

Florida	25
Louisiana	23
New Mexico	23
Oklahoma	23
Colorado	16
Arizona	15
New York	15
Idaho	11
Michigan	11
South Carolina	9
New Jersey	6
Maryland	5
Massachusetts	5
Nebraska	3
Nevada	3
Pennsylvania	3
Wisconsin	3
Wyoming	2
Dist. of Columbia	2
Delaware	1
Utah	1
West Virginia	1

Chapter Notes

ONE: The Immigrants

1. Sir Winston Churchill, *The Great Republic--A History of America*, ed. Winston S. Churchill (New York: Random House, 2000), 3-19.
2. Ibid., 23-24.
3. Ibid., 36-41.
4. Ibid., 42.
5. Ibid., 43.
6. David Freeman Hawke, *Everyday Life in Early America* (New York: Harper & Row, 1988; Perennial Library, 1989), 2.
7. Ibid., 5.
8. Ibid., 11.
9. Ibid., 12.
10. Ibid., 13.
11. Churchill, *Great Republic*, 44-45.
12. Angie Debo, *A History of the Indians of the United States* (Norman: The University of Oklahoma Press, 1983), 40.
13. Virginia Baker Mitchell, *Gholson and Allied Families*, ed. Margaret Scruggs-Carruth (Dallas: n.p., 1950), Concerning Origins, 1.
14. Lothrop Withington, *Virginia Gleanings in England, Abstracts of 17th and 18th-Century English Wills and Administrations Relating to Virginia and Virginians: A Consolidation of Articles from The Virginia Magazine of History and Biography* (Baltimore: Genealogical Publishing Co., 1980), 120-1.
15. John Venn and J. A. Venn, comp., *Alumni Cantabrigienses: A Biographical List of All Known Students, Graduates and Holders of Office at the University of Cambridge, From the Earliest Times to 1900, Part I, From the Earliest Times to 1751, Volume II, Dabbs-Juxton* (Cambridge: At the University Press, 1922), 273.
16. Susan Myra Kingsbury, ed., *Heritage Books Archives: Records of the Virginia Company of London, Volumes 1-4*, CD (Bowie, MD: Heritage Books Archives, 1999) pdf vii, 215 ff.
17. The Rev. Silas Emmett Lucas, Jr., *Virginia Colonial Abstracts--Series 2, Vol. 3: The Virginia Company of London, 1607-1624*, abstr. and comp. Beverley Fleet, ed. The Rev. Lindsay O. Duvall (Easley, SC: Southern Historical Press, 1978), 38.
18. Hawke, *Everyday Life*, 6.
19. Ibid., 9.
20. Ibid.
21. Lucas, *Virginia Colonial Abstracts*, 38.
22. Leslie Stephen and Sidney Lee, eds., *Dictionary of National Biography, Vol. 8, Glover-Harriott*, "Goulston or Gulston, Theodore, M.D." (New York: The McMillan Company, 1908), 289.
23. Withington, *Virginia Gleanings in England*, 120.
24. Venn and Venn, *Alumni Cantabrigienses*, 274.
25. Peter Wilson Coldham, *The Complete Book of Emigrants 1661-1699: A Comprehensive Listing Compiled from English Public Records of Those Who*

Took Ship to the Americas for Political, Religious, and Economic Reasons; of Those Who Were Deported for Vagrancy, Roguery, or Non-Conformity; and of Those Who Were Sold to Labour in the New Colonies (Baltimore: Genealogical Publishing Co., Inc., 1990), 238.

26. David Hackett Fischer, *Albion's Seed--Four British Folkways in America* (New York: Oxford University Press, 1989), 308.

27. Churchill, *Great Republic*, 44-45.

28. Ibid., 48-49.

29. Ibid., 50.

30. Ibid., 51.

31. Ibid., 52-55.

32. John C. Miller, ed., *The Colonial Image--Origins of American Culture* (New York: George Braziller, 1962), 15.

33. Ibid.

34. Thomas Sowell, *Conquests and Cultures--An International History* (New York: Basic Books, 1998), 80.

35. Francis Dillon, *The Pilgrims--Their Journeys & Their World* (Garden City, NJ: Doubleday & Company, Inc., 1975), 151.

36. Miller, *Colonial Image*, 86.

37. Ibid., 88.

38. Ibid.

39. Ibid., 86.

40. Ibid., 88.

41. Ibid., 86.

42. Ibid., 88-9.

43. Alden T. Vaughan, *America Before the Revolution 1725-1775* (Englewood Cliffs, New Jersey: Prentice-Hall, Inc., 1967), 5.

44. James E. Brown and Margaret Brown Altendahl, comps., *Relatives of the Browns of Mill Springs, Kentucky: Including the Fisher, Gaar, Gholson, Hutchison, Weaver and West Families* (Baltimore: Gateway Press, Inc., 1992), xxiii.

45. Mitchell, *Gholson and Allied Families*, Concerning Origins, 3.

46. New England Historic Genealogical Society, *The New-England Historical and Genealogical Register 1895, Vol. XLIX* (Boston: Published by The Society, 1895), 485.

47. John Camden Hotten, ed., *The Original Lists of Persons of Quality; Emigrants; Religious Exiles; Political Rebels; Serving Men Sold for a Term of Years; Apprentices; Children Stolen; Maidens Pressed; and Others Who Went from Great Britain to the American Plantations, 1600-1700, With Their Ages, The Localities Where They Formerly Lived in the Mother Country, The Names of the Ships in Which They Embarked, and Other Interesting Particulars, From MSS. Preserved in the State Paper Department of Her Majesty's Public Record Office, England* (Baltimore: Genealogical Publishing Co., Inc. 1968), 282, 284.

48. Nell Marion Nugent, abstr. and ind., *Cavaliers and Pioneers--Abstracts of Virginia Land Patents & Grants, 1623-1666, Vol. 1* (Baltimore: Genealogical Publishing Co., Inc., 1979), 131.

49. Miller, *Colonial Image*, 294.

50. Hawke, *Everyday Life*, 120.
51. Ibid., 123.
52. Ibid., 124.
53. Vaughan, *America Before the Revolution*, 43.
54. Churchill, *Great Republic*, 73.
55. Vaughan, *America Before the Revolution*, 6.
56. Brown & Altendahl, *Relatives of the Browns*, xxiii.
57. Ibid.
58. Churchill, *Great Republic*, 72-3.

TWO: Life in Early Virginia - 1600-1800

1. David Freeman Hawke, *Everyday Life in Early America* (New York: Harper & Row, 1988; Perennial Library, 1989), 13-15.
2. Ibid., 33.
3. Ibid., 36.
4. Ibid., 37.
5. Ibid., 38.
6. Ibid., 39.
7. Ibid., 40.
8. Ibid., 52.
9. Ibid., 55.
10. Ibid., 56.
11. Ibid., 57.
12. Ibid., 43-4.
13. Ibid., 44-5.
14. John C. Miller, ed., *The Colonial Image--Origins of American Culture* (New York: George Braziller, 1962), 297.
15. Ibid., 298.
16. Ibid., 297-9.
17. Ibid., 301.
18. Hawke, *Everyday Life*, 84.
19. Ibid., 84-5.
20. David Hackett Fischer, *Albion's Seed--Four British Folkways in America* (New York: Oxford University Press, 1989), 311.
21. Hawke, *Everyday Life*, 81.
22. Ibid., 82.
23. Ibid., 83.
24. Ibid., 21.
25. Fischer, *Albion's Seed*, 277.
26. William Armstrong Crozier, ed., *Virginia County Records, Spotsylvania County 1721-1800: Being Transcriptions, from the Original Files at the County Court House, of Wills, Deeds, Administrators' and Guardians' Bonds, Marriage Licenses, and Lists of Revolutionary Pensioners* (1905; reprint, Baltimore: Genealogical Publishing Co., Inc., 1978), 70.
27. James E. Brown and Margaret Brown Altendahl, comps., *Relatives of the Browns of Mill Springs, Kentucky, Including the Fisher, Gaar, Gholson, Hutchison,*

Weaver and West Families (Baltimore: Gateway Press, Inc., 1992), 104. From Spotsylvania County, Virginia O.B. (1724-1730), p. 324.

28. Augusta Phillips Johnson, *A Century of Wayne County, Kentucky, 1800-1900* (Louisville: The Standard Printing Company, Inc., 1939), 224.

29. F. B. Kegley, *Kegley's Virginia Frontier: The Beginning of the Southwest, The Roanoke of Colonial Days, 1740-1783, With Maps and Illustrations* (Roanoke: The Southwest Virginia Historical Society, 1938), 525-6.

30. Fischer, *Albion's Seed*, 326.

31. Ibid., 328.

32. Hawke, *Everyday Life*, 21-2.

33. Ibid., 61.

34. Ibid., 20.

35. Fischer, *Albion's Seed*, 210.

36. Paula S. Felder, *Forgotten Companions: The First Settlers of Spotsylvania County and Fredericksburgh Town (With Notes on Early Land Use)* (Fredericksburg, VA: Historic Publications of Fredericksburg, 1982), 52.

37. Fischer, *Albion's Seed*, 233-5.

38. Johnson, *Century of Wayne County*, 76. Anthony₁ also had a son named Anthony, often referred to in documents as Anthony, Jr. He was the brother of William, father of Anthony₂. This work contains only a few references to Anthony, Jr. pertaining to Anthony₁ and his son William.

39. Fischer, *Albion's Seed*, 257. [Many older Texans still use these expressions today. When Conner Gholson, my father, was asked by one of his friends how he was doing, his answer might have been "Porely." I was often told that I "favor" my father.]

40. Ibid., 261.

41. Ibid., 258.

42. Ibid., 259.

43. Ibid., 262.

44. Ibid., 259.

45. Virginia Baker Mitchell, *Gholson and Allied Families*, ed. Margaret Scruggs-Carruth (Dallas: n.p., 1950), Concerning Origins, 3.

46. Fischer, *Albion's Seed*, 345.

47. Ibid., 347.

48. Ibid., 347-8.

49. Ibid., 347.

50. Adrienne Koch and William Peden, eds., *The Life and Selected Writings of Thomas Jefferson* (1944; reprint, New York: Modern Library, 1998), 233.

51. Fischer, *Albion's Seed*, 281.

52. Ibid., 286.

53. Ibid., 298.

54. Ibid., 300.

55. Ibid., 302.

56. Ibid., 304.

57. Ibid., 283.

58. Hawke, *Everyday Life*, 63.

59. Koch and Peden, *Life and Selected Writings of Thomas Jefferson*, 455.
60. Carl Holliday, *Woman's Life in Colonial Days* (1922; reprint, Mineola, NY: Dover Publications, Inc., 1999), 74.
61. Ibid., 105.
62. Ibid., 106.
63. Ibid., 107.
64. Ibid., 113.
65. Ibid.
66. Ibid., 114.
67. Mitchell, *Gholson and Allied Families*, 3.
68. Ibid., 11.
69. Ibid., 15.
70. Holliday, *Woman's Life in Colonial Days*, 114.
71. Hawke, *Everyday Life*, 61.
72. Stephen E. Ambrose, *Undaunted Courage: Meriwether Lewis, Thomas Jefferson, and the Opening of the American West* (New York: Touchstone, 1996), 31-2.
73. June Baldwin Bork, compiler, *Wayne County, Kentucky, Deed Book D, 1823-1828* (Apple Valley, CA: June Baldwin Bork, 1994), 42.
74. Hawke, *Everyday Life*, 78.
75. Ibid., 79.
76. Miller, *Colonial Image*, 302.
77. Ibid., 302-3.
78. Ibid., 303-4.
79. Johnson, *Century of Wayne County*, 224.
80. Joyce and Richard Wolkomir, "When Bandogs Howle & Spirits Walk," *Smithsonian Magazine* 31, no. 10 (2001): 40.
81. Ibid.
82. Ibid.
83. Ibid., 40-41.
84. Ibid., 43.
85. Ibid., 44.
86. Brown and Altendahl, *Relatives of the Browns*, 105.
87. Ambrose, *Undaunted Courage*, 30.
88. Ibid.
89. Alden T. Vaughan, *America Before the Revolution 1725-1775* (Englewood Cliffs, NJ: Prentice-Hall, Inc., 1967), 165.
90. Ibid., 164.
91. Fischer, *Albion's Seed*, 343.
92. Ambrose, *Undaunted Courage*, 32.
93. Koch & Peden, *Life & Selected Writings of Thomas Jefferson*, 262.
94. Mitchell, *Gholson and Allied Families*, 14.
95. Kegley, *Kegley's Virginia Frontier*, 513.
96. Koch and Peden, *Life and Selected Writings of Thomas Jefferson*, 564.
97. Vaughan, *America Before the Revolution*, 157.
98. Fischer, *Albion's Seed*, 313.
99. Ibid., 349-54.

100. Ibid., 314.
101. Ibid., 315.
102. Hawke, *Everyday Life*, 8.
103. Ibid., 67.
104. Ibid., 68.
105. Ibid., 118.
106. Ibid., 119.
107. Ibid., 120.
108. Ambrose, *Undaunted Courage*, 55.
109. Hawke, *Everyday Life*, 127.
110. David Brion Davis and Steven Mintz, *The Boisterous Sea of Liberty: A Documentary History of America from Discovery Through the Civil War* (Oxford: Oxford University Press, 1998), 57.
111. Hawke, *Everyday Life*, 127.
112. Miller, *Colonial Image*, 20, 31.
113. Ibid., 31.
114. Ibid., 33.

THREE: Virginia – The Planters and the Land

1. Page Smith, *John Adams, Vol. I, 1735-1784* (Garden City, NY: Doubleday & Company, Inc., 1962), 51.
2. Ibid., 259.
3. Ibid., 272.
4. Alden T. Vaughan, *America Before the Revolution 1725-1775* (Englewood Cliffs, NJ: Prentice-Hall, Inc., 1967), 23.
5. Ulysses P. Joyner, Jr., *Orange County Land Patents*, 2d ed., (Orange County Historical Society, Inc., 1999), 7.
6. Ibid., 9.
7. Nell Marion Nugent, abstr. and ind., *Cavaliers and Pioneers--Abstracts of Virginia Land Patents & Grants, 1623-1666, Vol. 1* (Baltimore: Genealogical Publishing Co., Inc., 1979), xxiv.
8. James E. Brown and Margaret Brown Altendahl, comps., *Relatives of the Browns of Mill Springs, Kentucky, Including the Fisher, Gaar, Gholson, Hutchison, Weaver and West Families* (Baltimore: Gateway Press, Inc., 1992), xi.
9. Parke Rouse, Jr., *The Great Wagon Road: from Philadelphia To the South* (New York: McGraw-Hill, 1973), 12.
10. William Armstrong Crozier, ed., *Virginia County Records, Spotsylvania County 1721-1800; Transcriptions from the Original Files at the County Court House* (Baltimore: Genealogical Publishing Co., Inc., 1978), 95.
11. Ibid., 149.
12. Joyner, *Orange County Land Patents*, 27.
13. Virginia Baker Mitchell, *Gholson and Allied Families*, ed. Margaret Scruggs-Carruth (Dallas: n.p., 1950), 1.
14. Joyner, *Orange County Land Patents*, 27.
15. Mitchell, *Gholson and Allied Families*, 1.
16. Rouse, *Great Wagon Road*, 11.

17. Philip Vickers Fithian, *Journal & Letters of Philip Vickers Fithian, 1773-1774, A Plantation Tutor of the Old Dominion,* ed. Hunter Dickinson Farish (1943; reprint, Charlottesville: The University Press of Virginia, 1996), xv.

18. Joyner, *Orange County Land Patents,* 12.

19. Adrienne Koch and William Peden, eds., *The Life and Selected Writings of Thomas Jefferson* (1944; reprint, New York: Modern Library, 1998), 248.

20. Nathaniel Mason Pawlett, *Historic Roads of Virginia, Spotsylvania County Road Orders, 1722-1734* (Virginia Highway & Transportation Research Council, n.d.), 21.

21. Ibid., 39.

22. Ibid., 44. See Explanatory Notes regarding the calendar year.

23. Ibid., 45.

24. Ibid., 81.

25. Fithian, *Journal and Letters,* xv.

26. Brown and Altendahl, *Relatives of the Browns,* 107.

27. Ibid., 105.

28. Ibid., 106.

29. Ibid., 107.

30. Mitchell, *Gholson and Allied Families,* 10. See Chapter 6 for more about Captain Joseph Collins.

31. Ibid., 11.

32. Brown and Altendahl, *Relatives of the Browns,* 145.

33. Mitchell, *Gholson and Allied Families,* 11.

34. Ibid., 10.

35. Brown and Altendahl, *Relatives of the Browns,* 198.

36. W. W. Abbot and Dorothy Twohig, eds., *The Papers of George Washington, Colonial Series, Vol. 8, June 1767-December 1771* (Charlottesville: University Press of Virginia), 568, 570. Anthony's name also appears in Vol. 9, on pages 110, 503-4, in Washington's Cash Accounts records. William's brother Anthony, Jr. apparently died in 1779, so this note must refer to William's son Anthony.

37. "Virginia Legislative Papers; From Originals in The Virginia State Archives," *Virginia Magazine of History and Biography* 13, no. 4, (1906): 412. Berkeley County, West Virginia, was formed from a part of Frederick County in 1772, and Frederick County, Virginia, was formed from a part of Orange County in 1743.

38. Ibid., 413.

39. Ibid., 411.

40. Brown and Altendahl, *Relatives of the Browns,* 200.

41. John H. Gwathmey, *Historical Register of Virginians in the Revolution: Soldiers, Sailors, Marines; 1775-1783* (Baltimore: Genealogical Publishing Co., Inc., 1979), 314.

42. Lyman Chalkley, *Chronicles of the Scotch-Irish Settlement in Virginia, Extracted from the Original Court Records of Augusta County, 1745-1800, Vol. II* (1912; reprint, Baltimore: Genealogical Publishing Co., Inc., 1974), 423.

43. Brown and Altendahl, *Relatives of the Browns,* 200.

44. Virginia Genealogical Society, *Virginia Genealogical Society Quarterly* 13, no. 2, (1975): 33.

45.   Lewis Preston Summers, *Annals of Southwest Virginia, 1769-1800* (Abingdon, VA: Lewis Preston Summers, 1929), 377.

46.   Brown and Altendahl, *Relatives of the Browns*, 202-3.

47.   Summers, *Annals of Southwest Virginia*, 401.

48.   Ibid., 405.

49.   Ibid., 431.

50.   Ibid., 447.

51.   Mitchell, *Gholson and Allied Families*, 14.

52.   F. B. Kegley, *Kegley's Virginia Frontier: The Beginning of the Southwest, The Roanoke of Colonial Days, 1740-1783, With Maps and Illustrations* (Roanoke: The Southwest Virginia Historical Society, 1938), 520.

53.   David Freeman Hawke, *Everyday Life in Early America* (New York: Harper & Row, 1988; Perennial Library, 1989), 145.

54.   Ibid., 146.

55.   Mitchell, *Gholson and Allied Families*, 14.

56.   Kegley, *Kegley's Virginia Frontier*, 500.

57.   Hawke, *Everyday Life*, 146-7.

58.   Fithian, *Journal and Letters*, xiv.

59.   Rouse, *Great Wagon Road*, 227.

60.   Brown and Altendahl, *Relatives of the Browns*, xxvii.

61.   Mitchell, *Gholson and Allied Families*, 15.

62.   Ibid., 14.

63.   Ibid.

64.   Koch & Peden, *Life & Selected Writings of Thomas Jefferson*, xxxv.

FOUR: Virginians in the American Revolution

1.   David Brion Davis and Steven Mintz, *The Boisterous Sea of Liberty: A Documentary History of America from Discovery Through the Civil War* (Oxford: Oxford University Press, 1998), 3.

2.   E. M. Sanchez-Saavedra, comp., *A Guide to Virginia Military Organizations in the American Revolution, 1774-1787* (Richmond: Virginia State Library, 1978), vii.

3.   Sir Winston Churchill, *The Great Republic--A History of America*, Large Print version, ed. Winston S. Churchill (New York: Random House, 2000), 97-8.

4.   Ibid., 98-100.

5.   Ibid., 105-6.

6.   Ibid., 108.

7.   Ibid., 109-10.

8.   Ibid., 111-12.

9.   Philip Vickers Fithian, *Journal & Letters of Philip Vickers Fithian, 1773-1774, A Plantation Tutor of the Old Dominion*, ed. Hunter Dickinson Farish (1943; reprint, Charlottesville: The University Press of Virginia, 1996), 110.

10.   William H. Hallahan, *The Day the American Revolution Began: 19 April 1775* (New York: William Morrow and Company, 2000), 188-9.

11.   Ibid., 189.

12.   Ibid., 190.

13. Benson Bobrick, *Angel in the Whirlwind: The Triumph of the American Revolution* (New York: Simon & Schuster, Inc., 1997; New York: Penguin Putnam Inc., 1998), 110.

14. Hallahan, *Day the American Revolution Began*, 190.

15. Ibid., 191.

16. Ibid.

17. Ibid., 192.

18. Churchill, *Great Republic*, 112-13.

19. Hallahan, *Day the American Revolution Began*, 177.

20. Bobrick, *Angel in the Whirlwind*, 123.

21. Ibid., 124.

22. Hallahan, *Day the American Revolution Began*, 183-4.

23. Ibid., 184.

24. Ibid., 195.

25. Ibid., 196.

26. Hallahan, *Day the American Revolution Began*, 184.

27. Ibid., 185.

28. Ibid., 197.

29. Ibid.

30. Sanchez-Saavedra, *Guide to Virginia Military Organizations*, 137.

31. Ibid.

32. Joyce Lee Malcolm, *To Keep and Bear Arms, The Origins of an Anglo-American Right* (Cambridge, MA: Harvard University Press, 1994), 138.

33. Ibid., 140.

34. Ibid.

35. Ibid., 139.

36. Adrienne Koch and William Peden, eds., *The Life and Selected Writings of Thomas Jefferson* (1944; reprint, New York: Modern Library, 1998), 205-6.

37. Malcolm, *To Keep and Bear Arms*, 143.

38. Ibid., 144.

39. Ibid., 145.

40. Hallahan, *Day the American Revolution Began*, 198.

41. Ibid., 199.

42. Ibid., 205.

43. Koch and Peden, *Life & Selected Writings of Thomas Jefferson*, xxi.

44. Davis and Mintz, *Boisterous Sea of Liberty*, 203.

45. Virginia Baker Mitchell, *Gholson and Allied Families*, ed. Margaret Scruggs-Carruth (Dallas: n.p., 1950), 14.

46. John H. Gwathmey, *Historical Register of Virginians in the Revolution: Soldiers, Sailors, Marines; 1775-1783* (Baltimore: Genealogical Publishing Co., Inc., 1979), 314.

47. James E. Brown and Margaret Brown Altendahl, comps., *Relatives of the Browns of Mill Springs, Kentucky, Including the Fisher, Gaar, Gholson, Hutchison, Weaver and West Families* (Baltimore: Gateway Press, Inc., 1992), xvi.

48. Virginia Genealogical Society, *Virginia Genealogical Society Quarterly* 13, no. 2, (1975): 33.

49. Bobrick, *Angel in the Whirlwind*, 432.
50. *DAR Patriot Index, Centennial Edition*, Part II (Washington: National Society of the Daughters of the American Revolution, 1994), 1182.

FIVE: Over the Mountains to Kentucky

1. Frederick Jackson Turner, *The Frontier in American History* (1920; reprint, New York: Dover Publications, 1996), 37.
2. Robert L. Kincaid, *The Wilderness Road* (Indianapolis: The Bobbs-Merrill Company, 1947), 73.
3. Parke Rouse, Jr., *The Great Wagon Road: from Philadelphia To the South* (New York: McGraw-Hill, 1973), 107-8.
4. Kincaid, *Wilderness Road*, 74-5.
5. Ibid., 75-6.
6. Ibid., 78.
7. Ibid., 78-9.
8. Ibid., 80.
9. Ibid., 82-90.
10. Ibid., 98.
11. Ibid., 99.
12. Ibid., 100-101.
13. Ibid., 102-3.
14. Ibid., 103-4.
15. Ibid., 105.
16. Ibid., 106-7.
17. Ibid.
18. Ibid., 110.
19. Rouse, *Great Wagon Road*, 110.
20. Ibid., 112.
21. Ibid., 116.
22. Kincaid, *Wilderness Road*, 184.
23. Ibid., 185.
24. Ibid., 186.
25. Ibid., 187.
26. Ibid., 188.
27. Ibid., 189.
28. Ibid., 190.
29. Ibid., 191.
30. Virginia Baker Mitchell, *Gholson and Allied Families*, ed. Margaret Scruggs-Carruth (Dallas: n.p., 1950), 15.
31. Kincaid, *Wilderness Road*, 188.
32. Ibid., 192.
33. Augusta Phillips Johnson, *A Century of Wayne County, Kentucky, 1800-1900* (Louisville: The Standard Printing Company, Inc., 1939), 22.
34. Ibid., 24.
35. Ibid., 25.
36. Ibid., 21.

37.   Ibid., 22-3, 28.

38.   Ibid., 28-9.

39.   James E. Brown and Margaret Brown Altendahl, comps., *Relatives of the Browns of Mill Springs, Kentucky, Including the Fisher, Gaar, Gholson, Hutchison, Weaver and West Families* (Baltimore: Gateway Press, Inc., 1992), 198.

40.   Johnson, *Century of Wayne County*, 34.

41.   Ibid., 35.

42.   Ibid.

43.   Brown and Altendahl, *Relatives of the Browns*, 204.

44.   Sara Belle Upchurch, ed., "Anthony Gholson House," *Wayne County Historical Society Overview* 18, no. 1 (1997).

45.   Ibid.

46.   Brown and Altendahl, *Relatives of the Browns*, 206.

47.   June Baldwin Bork, comp., *Wayne County, Kentucky, Deed Book B, 1811-1818* (Apple Valley, CA: June Baldwin Bork, 1993), 54.

48.   Johnson, *Century of Wayne County*, 76.

49.   Eric Sloane, *Diary of an Early American Boy: Noah Blake, 1805* (New York: Wilfred Funk, Inc., 1965; New York: Ballantine Books, 1974), 18.

50.   Bork, *Wayne County, Kentucky, Deed Book B*, 54.

51.   Anthony Gholson Biography, Gholson Family File, Wayne County Historical Society, Monticello, Kentucky.

52.   Mitchell, *Gholson and Allied Families*, 15.

53.   Turner, *Frontier in American History*, 19.

54.   Ibid., 20.

55.   Ibid., 21.

SIX: The Family of Anthony$_2$ Gholson of Virginia and Kentucky

56.   James E. Brown and Margaret Brown Altendahl, comps., *Relatives of the Browns of Mill Springs, Kentucky, Including the Fisher, Gaar, Gholson, Hutchison, Weaver and West Families* (Baltimore: Gateway Press, Inc., 1992), 88.

57.   Benson Bobrick, *Angel in the Whirlwind: The Triumph of the American Revolution* (New York: Simon & Schuster, Inc., 1997; New York: Penguin Putnam Inc., 1998), 28-9.

58.   Brown and Altendahl, *Relatives of the Browns*, 90.

59.   Ibid., 90-91.

60.   Micah Taul Memoirs TS, No. 778, Papers of Bennett Henderson Young, 1879-1912, A\Y68, The Filson Club, Louisville, KY, 58.

61.   Adjutant General of the State of Kentucky, *Soldiers of the War of 1812* (Frankfort, 1891), 154.

62.   Taul Memoirs, 55.

63.   Ibid., 1-3.

64.   Ibid., 12.

65.   Ibid.

66.   Ibid., 5.

67   Ibid., 12.

68.   Ibid., 13.

69.   Ibid., 14-15.
70.   Ibid., 15.
71.   Ibid., 38.
72.   Ibid., 16-17.
73.   Ibid., 22.
74.   Ibid., 23.
75.   Ibid., 26.
76.   Ibid., 27.
77.   Ibid., 28.
78.   Ibid., 29.
79.   Ibid., 31-32. Some typographical errors corrected.
80.   Ibid., 32.
81.   Ibid., 33.
82.   Ibid., 34.
83.   Ibid., 34-5.
84.   Ibid., 39.
85.   Ibid.
86.   Ibid.
87.   Ibid., 62-5.
88.   Ibid., 66.
89.   Ibid., 66-7.
90.   Ibid., 67.
91.   Ibid.
92.   Ibid., 68.
93.   Ibid., 69.
94.   Ibid., 70.
95.   Ibid.
96.   Ibid., 71.
97.   Ibid., 72.
98.   Ibid.
99.   Ibid.
100.   Ibid., 73.
101.   Ibid.
102.   Ibid., 74.
103.   Ibid.
104.   Ibid., 75.
105.   Ibid., 76.
106.   Ibid., 77.
107.   Augusta Phillips Johnson, *A Century of Wayne County, Kentucky, 1800-1900* (Louisville: The Standard Printing Co., 1939), 38.
108.   Taul Memoirs, 77.
109.   Johnson, *A Century of Wayne County, Kentucky*, 224.
110.   Taul Memoirs, 78.
111.   Ibid., 79.
112.   Ibid., 80-81.
113.   Ibid., 82.

114. Ibid., 87.
115. Ibid.
116. Ibid., 88.
117. Ibid., 88-9.
118. Ibid., 89-90.
119. Ibid., 91.
120. Ibid.
121. Ibid., 92.
122. Ibid., 93.
123. Ibid., 94.
124. Ibid., 95.
125. Ibid., 99.
126. Ibid., 99-100.
127. Ibid., 100.
128. Ibid., 101.
129. Ibid., 106.
130. Ibid., addendum page 4.
131. Ibid., addendum page 27.
132. Ibid., addendum page 32.
133. Brown and Altendahl, *Relatives of the Browns*, 280.
134. Ibid., 198.
135. Ibid.
136. Taul Memoirs, 29.
137. Brown and Altendahl, *Relatives of the Browns*, 198.

SEVEN: Kentuckians in the War of 1812

1. Donald R. Hickey, *The War of 1812: A Forgotten Conflict* (Urbana, IL: University of Illinois Press, 1990), 72.
2. Ibid., 73.
3. Micah Taul Memoirs TS, No. 778, Papers of Bennett Henderson Young, 1879-1912, A\Y68, The Filson Club, Louisville, KY, 22.
4. David Brion Davis and Steven Mintz, *The Boisterous Sea of Liberty: A Documentary History of America from Discovery Through the Civil War* (Oxford: Oxford University Press, 1998), 305.
5. Hickey, *War of 1812*, 30.
6. Ibid., 46.
7. James E. Brown and Margaret Brown Altendahl, comps., *Relatives of the Browns of Mill Springs, Kentucky, Including the Fisher, Gaar, Gholson, Hutchison, Weaver and West Families* (Baltimore: Gateway Press, Inc., 1992), 198.
8. Taul Memoirs, 40.
9. Ibid., 47. This company may or may not have included Dorothy's brother Samuel. See note 29 below. The source gives an 1813 enlistment date for Samuel.
10. Hickey, *War of 1812*, 80.
11. Ibid., 82, 84.
12. Taul Memoirs, 48.

13. Ibid., 53.
14. Ibid.
15. Hickey, *War of 1812*, 85.
16. C. Edward Skeen, *Citizen Soldiers in the War of 1812* (Lexington: The University Press of Kentucky, 1999), 83.
17. Hickey, *War of 1812*, 85.
18. Taul Memoirs, 53.
19. Ibid.
20. Ibid., 54.
21. Ibid., 55.
22. Ibid., 56.
23. Ibid.
24. Hickey, *War of 1812*, 126.
25. Taul Memoirs, 57.
26. Brown and Altendahl, *Relatives of the Browns*, 198. Bartholomew Haden was married to Anthony$_2$ Gholson's daughter Catherine, the sister of Micah's wife.
27. Adjutant General of the State of Kentucky, *Soldiers of the War of 1812* (Frankfort, 1891), 154.
28. Taul Memoirs, 57.
29. Hickey, *War of 1812*, 127.
30. Ibid., 128.
31. Ibid., 131.
32. Ibid., 132.
33. Ibid., 133.
34. Ibid., 135.
35. John R. Elting, *Amateurs, To Arms! A Military History of the War of 1812* (Chapel Hill, NC: Algonquin Books, 1991; Da Capo Press, Inc., 1995), 98.
36. National Archives, Military Service Records, NWCTB Master No. 542698, SOP No. 150198.
37. Taul Memoirs, 59.
38. Ibid.
39. Ibid.
40. Hickey, *War of 1812*, 79.
41. Ibid.
42. Taul Memoirs, 59-60.
43. Ibid., 60.
44. Hickey, *War of 1812*, 137.
45. Gerard T. Altoff, *Oliver Hazard Perry and the Battle of Lake Erie* (Put-in-Bay, Ohio: The Perry Group, 1999), 59.
46. Ibid., 61.
47. Hickey, *War of 1812*, 137-9.
48. Altoff, *Perry and the Battle of Lake Erie*, 64-5.
49. Elting, *Amateurs, to Arms*, 113.
50. Hickey, *War of 1812*, 139.
51. Taul Memoirs, 61.
52. Hickey, *War of 1812*, 139.

53. Altoff, *Perry and the Battle of Lake Erie*, 65-6.
54. Taul Memoirs, 62.
55. Hickey, *War of 1812*, 182-3.
56. Ibid., 196.
57. Ibid., 198-9.
58. Ibid., 203-4.
59. Ibid., 204-5.
60. Ibid., 206.
61. Leonard V. Huber, *The Battle of New Orleans: New Orleans as it was in 1814-1815* (New Orleans: Battle of New Orleans 150th Anniversary Committee of Louisiana, 1965; reprint, New Orleans: Louisiana Landmarks Society, 1994), 3.
62. Ibid., 8-10.
63. Ibid., 38-9.
64. Hickey, *War of 1812*, 206.
65. Ibid., 207.
66. Ibid., 209.
67. Ibid., 209-10.
68. Ibid., 210.
69. Sir Winston Churchill, *The Great Republic--A History of America*, Large Print version, ed. Winston S. Churchill (New York: Random House, 2000), 208.
70. Hickey, *War of 1812*, 211-12.
71. Adjutant General, Kentucky, *Soldiers of the War of 1812*, 291-2.
72. Augusta Phillips Johnson, *A Century of Wayne County, Kentucky, 1800-1900* (Louisville: The Standard Printing Co., 1939), 60.
73. Skeen, *Citizen Soldiers in the War of 1812*, 171.
74. Ibid.
75. Hickey, *War of 1812*, 288.
76. Ibid., 212.
77. Hickey, *War of 1812*, 2.
78. Taul Memoirs, 62.
79. Hickey, *War of 1812*, 3.

EIGHT: Chasing Gholson Ghosts

Personal experiences and photographs of Donna Gholson Cook's road trip through Virginia and Kentucky to visit the locations of her Gholson ancestors.

Bibliography

Abbot, W. W., and Dorothy Twohig, eds. *The Papers of George Washington, Colonial Series, Vol. 8, June 1767-December 1771.* Charlottesville: University Press of Virginia.

Altoff, Gerard T. *Oliver Hazard Perry and the Battle of Lake Erie.* Put-in-Bay, Ohio: The Perry Group, 1999.

Ambrose, Stephen E. *Undaunted Courage: Meriwether Lewis, Thomas Jefferson, and the Opening of the American West.* New York: Touchstone, 1996.

Another Researchers Publication. *Wayne County, Kentucky, Marriages, 1800-1850.* N.p., n.d.

Bobrick, Benson. *Angel in the Whirlwind: The Triumph of the American Revolution.* New York: Simon & Schuster, Inc., 1997; New York: Penguin Putnam Inc., 1998.

Bork, June Baldwin, comp. *Wayne County, Kentucky, Marriages and Vital Records; Deed Books A-E.* Apple Valley, CA: June Baldwin Bork, 1994.

Brown, James E., and Margaret Brown Altendahl, comps. *Relatives of the Browns of Mill Springs, Kentucky: Including the Fisher, Gaar, Gholson, Hutchison, Weaver and West Families.* Baltimore: Gateway Press, Inc., 1992.

Census Records of the United States.

Chalkley, Lyman. *Chronicles of the Scotch-Irish Settlement in Virginia, Extracted from the Original Court Records of Augusta County, 1745-1800, Vol. II.* 1912; reprint, Baltimore: Genealogical Publishing Co., Inc., 1974.

Churchill, Sir Winston. *The Great Republic--A History of America,* Large Print version. Edited by Winston S. Churchill. New York: Random House, 2000.

Coldham, Peter Wilson. *The Complete Book of Emigrants 1661-1699: A Comprehensive Listing Compiled from English Public Records of Those Who Took Ship to the Americas for Political, Religious, and Economic Reasons; of Those Who Were Deported for Vagrancy, Roguery, or Non-Conformity; and of Those Who Were Sold to Labour in the New Colonies.* Baltimore: Genealogical Publishing Co., Inc., 1990.

Crozier, William Armstrong, ed. *Virginia County Records, Spotsylvania County 1721-1800: Being Transcriptions, from the Original Files at* the County Court House, of Wills, Deeds, Administrators' and Guardians' Bonds, Marriage Licenses, and Lists of Revolutionary Pensioners. 1905; reprint, Baltimore: Genealogical Publishing Co., Inc., 1978.

DAR Patriot Index, Centennial Edition, Part II. Washington: National Society of the Daughters of the American Revolution, 1994.

Davis, David Brion, and Steven Mintz. *The Boisterous Sea of Liberty: A Documentary History of America from Discovery Through the Civil War.* Oxford: Oxford University Press, 1998.

Debo, Angie. *A History of the Indians of the United States.* Norman: The University of Oklahoma Press, 1983.

Dillon, Francis. *The Pilgrims--Their Journeys & Their World.* Garden City, NJ: Doubleday & Company, Inc., 1975.

Elting, John R. *Amateurs, To Arms! A Military History of the War of 1812.* Chapel Hill, NC: Algonquin Books, 1991; Da Capo Press, Inc., 1995.

Felder, Paula S. *Forgotten Companions: The First Settlers of Spotsylvania County and Fredericksburgh Town (With Notes on Early Land Use).* Fredericksburg, VA: Historic Publications of Fredericksburg, 1982.

Fischer, David Hackett. *Albion's Seed--Four British Folkways in America.* New York: Oxford University Press, 1989.

Fithian, Philip Vickers. *Journal & Letters of Philip Vickers Fithian, 1773-1774, A Plantation Tutor of the Old Dominion.* Edited by Hunter Dickinson Farish. 1943; reprint, Charlottesville: The University Press of Virginia, 1996.

Gholson, Anthony, Biography. Gholson Family File. Wayne County Historical Society, Monticello, Kentucky.

Gholson, Ronald Lee, comp. *Gholson and Allied Families, A Revised Golden Anniversary Edition, Reprint of "Gholson and Allied Families" by Virginia Baker Mitchell, September, 1950.* Mulberry, IN: Ron Gholson, 2002.

Gwathmey, John H. *Historical Register of Virginians in the Revolution: Soldiers, Sailors, Marines; 1775-1783.* Baltimore: Genealogical Publishing Co., Inc., 1979.

Hallahan, William H. *The Day the American Revolution Began: 19 April 1775.* New York: William Morrow and Company, 2000.

Hawke, David Freeman. *Everyday Life in Early America.* New York: Harper & Row, 1988; Perennial Library, 1989.

Hickey, Donald R. *The War of 1812: A Forgotten Conflict.* Urbana, IL: University of Illinois Press, 1990.

Holliday, Carl. *Woman's Life in Colonial Days.* 1922; reprint, Mineola, NY: Dover Publications, Inc., 1999.

Hotten, John Camden, ed. *The Original Lists of Persons of Quality; Emigrants; Religious Exiles; Political Rebels; Serving Men Sold for a Term of Years; Apprentices; Children Stolen; Maidens Pressed; and Others Who Went from Great Britain to the American Plantations, 1600-1700, With Their Ages, The Localities Where They Formerly Lived in the Mother Country, The Names of the Ships in Which They Embarked, and Other Interesting Particulars, From MSS. Preserved in the State Paper Department of Her Majesty's Public Record Office, England.* Baltimore: Genealogical Publishing Co., Inc. 1968.

Huber, Leonard V. *The Battle of New Orleans: New Orleans as it was in 1814-1815.* New Orleans: Battle of New Orleans 150th Anniversary Committee of Louisiana, 1965; reprint, New Orleans: Louisiana Landmarks Society, 1994.

Johnson, Augusta Phillips. *A Century of Wayne County, Kentucky, 1800-1900.* Louisville: The Standard Printing Company, Inc., 1939.

Joyner, Ulysses P., Jr. *Orange County Land Patents.* 2nd ed. Orange County Historical Society, Inc., VA, 1999.

Kegley, F. B. *Kegley's Virginia Frontier: The Beginning of the Southwest, The Roanoke of Colonial Days, 1740-1783, With Maps and Illustrations.* Roanoke: The Southwest Virginia Historical Society, 1938.

Kentucky, Adjutant General of the State of. *Soldiers of the War of 1812.* Frankfort, 1891.

Kincaid, Robert L. *The Wilderness Road.* Indianapolis: The Bobbs-Merrill Company, 1947.

Kingsbury, Susan Myra, ed. *Heritage Books Archives: Records of the Virginia Company of London, Volumes 1-4*, CD. Bowie, MD: Heritage Books Archives, 1999.

Koch, Adrienne, and William Peden, eds. *The Life and Selected Writings of Thomas Jefferson.* 1944; reprint, New York: Modern Library, 1998.

Lucas, The Rev. Silas Emmett, Jr. *Virginia Colonial Abstracts--Series 2, Vol. 3: The Virginia Company of London, 1607-1624.* Abstracted and compiled by Beverley Fleet. Edited by The Rev. Lindsay O. Duvall. Easley, SC: Southern Historical Press, 1978.

Malcolm, Joyce Lee. *To Keep and Bear Arms, The Origins of an Anglo-American Right.* Cambridge, MA: Harvard University Press, 1994.

Midwest Tennessee Genealogical Society. "Abstracts from Early Madison County, Tennessee, Newspapers: *Jackson Gazette*, March 21, 1829."

Family Findings, 4, nos. 3-4 (1972); from TN GenWeb. http://www.tngenweb.org/madison/records/gazette.htm.

Miller, John C., ed. *The Colonial Image--Origins of American Culture.* New York: George Braziller, 1962.

Mitchell, Virginia Baker. *Gholson and Allied Families.* Edited by Margaret Scruggs-Carruth. Dallas: n.p., 1950.

National Archives. Military Service Records.

New England Historic Genealogical Society. *The New-England Historical and Genealogical Register 1895, Vol. XLIX.* Boston: Published by The Society, 1895.

Nugent, Nell Marion, abstr. and ind. *Cavaliers and Pioneers--Abstracts of Virginia Land Patents & Grants, 1623-1666, Vol. 1.* Baltimore: Genealogical Publishing Co., Inc., 1979.

Nutter, Mildred Moody, contrib. "Wayne County, Kentucky Miscellaneous Court Papers from Box File." *The Kentucky Genealogist* 20, no. 2 (1978).

Pawlett, Nathaniel Mason. *Historic Roads of Virginia, Spotsylvania County Road Orders, 1722-1734.* Virginia Highway & Transportation Research Council, n.d.

Rouse, Parke, Jr. *The Great Wagon Road: from Philadelphia To the South.* New York: McGraw-Hill, 1973.

S-K Publications. *Census Images, 1810-1820-1830-1840, Livingston County, Kentucky.* CD. Wichita, KS: S-K Publications, 2001.

Sanchez-Saavedra, E. M., comp. *A Guide to Virginia Military Organizations in the American Revolution, 1774-1787.* Richmond: Virginia State Library, 1978.

Sistler, Byron, and Barbara Sistler, comps. and eds. *Madison County, Tennessee, Marriages 1838-71.* Nashville: n.p., 1983.

Skeen, C. Edward. *Citizen Soldiers in the War of 1812.* Lexington: The University Press of Kentucky, 1999.

Sloane, Eric. *Diary of an Early American Boy: Noah Blake, 1805.* New York: Wilfred Funk, Inc., 1965; New York: Ballantine Books, 1974).

Smith, Page. *John Adams, Vol. I, 1735-1784.* Garden City, NY: Doubleday & Company, Inc., 1962.

Sowell, Thomas. *Conquests and Cultures--An International History.* New York: Basic Books, 1998.

Stephen, Leslie, and Sidney Lee, eds. *Dictionary of National Biography, Vol. 8, Glover-Harriott,* "Goulston or Gulston, Theodore, M.D." New York: The McMillan Company, 1908.

Summers, Lewis Preston. *Annals of Southwest Virginia, 1769-1800.* Abingdon, VA: Lewis Preston Summers, 1929.

Taul, Micah, Memoirs. TS, No. 778, Papers of Bennett Henderson Young, 1879-1912, A\Y68. The Filson Club, Louisville, KY.

Turner, Frederick Jackson. *The Frontier in American History.* 1920; reprint, New York: Dover Publications, 1996.

Upchurch, Sara Belle, ed. "Anthony Gholson House." *Wayne County Historical Society Overview* 18, no. 1 (1997).

Vaughan, Alden T. *America Before the Revolution 1725-1775.* Englewood Cliffs, NJ: Prentice-Hall, Inc., 1967.

Venn, John, and J. A. Venn, comps. *Alumni Cantabrigienses: A Biographical List of All Known Students, Graduates and Holders of Office at the University of Cambridge, From the Earliest Times to 1900, Part I, From the Earliest Times to 1751, Volume II, Dabbs-Juxton.* Cambridge: At the University Press, 1922.

"Virginia Legislative Papers; From Originals in The Virginia State Archives." *Virginia Magazine of History and Biography* 13, no. 4 (1906).

Withington, Lothrop. *Virginia Gleanings in England, Abstracts of 17th and 18th-Century English Wills and Administrations Relating to Virginia and Virginians: A Consolidation of Articles from The Virginia Magazine of History and Biography.* Baltimore: Genealogical Publishing Co., 1980.

Wolkomir, Joyce, and Richard Wolkomir. "When Bandogs Howle & Spirits Walk." *Smithsonian Magazine* 31, no. 10 (2001).

Index

ABOOKS

ALIVE Book Publishing and ALIVE Publishing Group
are imprints of Advanced Publishing LLC,
3200 A Danville Blvd., Suite 204, Alamo, California 94507

Telephone: 925.837.7303
alivebookpublishing.com

www.ingramcontent.com/pod-product-compliance
Lightning Source LLC
Chambersburg PA
CBHW050642150426
42813CB00054B/1162